RV SNOWBIRDING 101

BY MARSHA SPINK

Order this book online at www.trafford.com
or email orders@trafford.com

Most Trafford titles are also available at major online book retailers.

Printed in the United States of America.

ISBN: 978-1-4251-7494-1 (sc)
ISBN: 978-1-4251-7495-8 (e)

Trafford rev. 06/17/2011

www.trafford.com

North America & international
toll-free: 1 888 232 4444 (USA & Canada)
phone: 250 383 6864 ♦ fax: 812 355 4082

TO PAUL

The Wind Beneath My Wings

Contributors

David Loewen, Phil Loewen, Patrick Spink, Laura Krowchenko	– Technical Advisors
Danielle Conrad	– Proof Reader
Paul Spink	– Editor, Photographer
Kersti Livingstone, Kathryn Livingstone	– Cover Artists

TABLE OF CONTENTS

THE GREAT ESCAPE

In a perfect world persons over fifty living north of Interstate 40 would winter in Maui, facing the turquoise channel to Molokai, surrounded by swaying palms and sweet-smelling plumeria. Days would be passed on the lanai with mai tais and pina coladas, on the golf course with spectacular ocean vistas, and on the sand with warm surf lapping at your feet.

In the real world winter escapees are more likely to follow the sun to the deserts of California or Arizona, the southern tip of Texas, or the beaches of Florida or Mexico. Some settle for the mild winters of the West Coast. A few succumb to the lure of the South Pacific, although probably only once or twice.

At a teachers' retirement banquet we attended not too long ago a large number of the new retirees stated they wanted to "travel, travel, travel". With today's trend towards early retirement, more and more are able to boldly go while they are still young and healthy. What better time to head out than during our most inhospitable season?

To most Canadians, snowbirds are a group of performing aircraft. The original dictionary definition refers to several varieties of thrushes, juncos, or buntings—common in snowy regions. It seems that Anne Murray's *Snowbird*, who flies *"to that land of gentle breezes where the peaceful waters flow"*, is the precursor to the term applying to persons who take flight to an idyllic place in the winter—to a more tropical destination than the aforementioned feathered variety. Some think a more fitting name would be "sunbird".

The exact parameters of how old, how warm, how far, and for how long, have not, to my knowledge, ever been discussed on 20/20, at Harvard, or in a barroom brawl. Statistics Canada sees a snowbird as a person 55 or older who spends more than 21 winter days in the United States. The definition used by the Canadian Snowbird Association is "any person who leaves Canada for at least 60 consecutive days". Most workable is the description used by MSN Encarta —"a winter traveler to a warmer climate".

In spite of the high cost of fuel and out-of-country insurance, plus low interest rates on retirement savings, snowbirds are a growing segment of our society, the Canadian Snowbird Association estimating about one and a half million annually flee from Canadian winters. The silver tsunami of baby boomers will soon further swell the snowbird ranks.

Except perhaps for skiers, who would not want to be a snowbird when they grow up?

Snowbirds on Wheels

Sometimes they fly, but usually they drive. Often they take their home with them. The advantages of traveling in a recreation vehicle are many.

Your money goes further, especially if you already own an RV. Even if you have to purchase, over the years the savings on extended winter vacations will be substantial. Most RV's are cheaper than a Sunbelt condominium and far more versatile.

Accommodations will be superior to your average motel unit or rental condo. You don't have to worry about cockroaches, bedbugs, a smoky room, a dirty bedspread, or ground floor rooms where you keep your drapes pulled and a chair in front of the door. You sleep in your own bed. Surrounded by nature if you choose.

RV meals are much cheaper, more nourishing, and probably tastier than at Denny's. You can avoid MSG, salt, and trans fats, and cater to special diets. In Mexico you can eat salads. Wine will not cost $9 a glass.

RV travel is independent travel. You can go where you want, when you want, with all the comforts of home. A clean washroom is always close at hand. If you are delayed en route or can't get a reservation, you can sleep in a parking lot. No matter how extensive your travels you unpack only once.

You avoid long waits and security hassles at the airport and see a lot more than at 35,000 feet. Delays and unexpected turbulence will be minimal, and the threat of terrorism and superbugs highly unlikely. There will be no surcharges and your luggage will not go astray.

Flexsteel captain chairs are far more comfortable than economy seats on a 737.

RV travel is the easiest mode for mobility-challenged passengers. You can take your pet. There is lots of room to pack treasures from outlet malls and swap meets. For outdoor enthusiasts it is the only way to go.

In the non-snowbird seasons you can continue to holiday economically, rent out your rig, or use it as an office or guest house.

RVing is good for your health. In an extensive study on the RV community, anthropologists David and Dorothy Counts found RVers to be "physically and mentally healthier, happier, and more alert than their retired counterparts who lead more sedentary lives".

This book studies all aspects of wintering in a warm climate in a recreational vehicle—the ideal RV, preparations, destinations, routes, parks, campground memberships, clubs, pets, lifestyles, and challenges, plus gives further reference sources. From a budget-minded, Canadian perspective. Unless noted, prices are for the year 2011 and in Canadian dollars when referring to purchases in Canada, and in American dollars for the U.S. Keep in mind that things change—in the RV world notably prices, businesses, and technology.

The key players are Marsha, Paul, and their faithful dog Simba, who traveled extensively in a 35' Bounder (two years as full-timers), a 30' Class C Yellowstone, and a 29' Itasca Sonova. We visited Florida, Texas, and Mexico twice, Arizona and California countless times, and toured New Zealand in a "campervan" (not Simba). We also lived on Canada's Riviera, Vancouver Island, for four years.

I hope our experiences can be an inspiration for you to take off from the Great White North and a help in launching or enhancing your winter escape.

Rigs and Toads

To be a member of the RVing contingent of snowbird society you gotta have a "rig", which is the terminology among the brotherhood for a home on wheels.

Most RV snowbirds have a history of "camping", but four months down south is quite different from two days at the lake. The weekender RV is designed for families and to sleep as many as possible. The long-term recreational vehicle is based on livability and comfort for two, the dinette and/or sofa available for the occasional overnight guest. For snowbirds, room for six for cocktails, four for dinner, and two for sleeping is considered ideal.

Would-be snowbirds with no camping experience should try to rent or borrow a rig before purchasing, although because of the complexity in coordinating with a towing vehicle, trailers and fifth wheels are seldom available for rental.

We have seen snowbirds in a tent trailer and neighbours from Parksville spent winters in Yuma in a truck camper. For most, such accommodations would be too cramped for a lengthy period, however, and some RV parks will not accept them. Because of their infrequency in snowbird locales, these compact options are not included in the following discussion.

With hundreds of models of recreational vehicles available, prospective buyers should research RV periodicals, buyers' guides, classified ads, the Internet, tradeshows, dealerships, owners, and RV lifestyle conferences. And take notes.

The first decision should be whether you want a towable RV or a motorhome.

Non-motorized (Towable)

Having no drive-train, trailers and fifth wheels are less expensive and retain their value better than motorhomes. With the living area separate from the driving cab they are more homelike and, with up to five slideouts, can be quite roomy. Once parked, the towing vehicle is freed for shopping and sightseeing.

On the downside, they can be difficult to maneuver on the road and to set up, have no direct access from the towing vehicle, lack built-in propane tanks and generators, and when camping in the wilderness you will have to go through the hitching/unhitching procedure at regular intervals to empty waste tanks and replenish water. It is against the law to occupy a trailer in transit.

Compatibility of size and style between the towing and towed units is imperative, as is adherence to the gross combined weight rating. The manufacturer's guide will determine the adequacy of the power, brakes, gear ratio, and weight of the proposed towing vehicle. B.C. law requires it have at least one horsepower for each 150 kg of the total weight of the truck/trailer (/fifth wheel) combination. Other provinces and states have similar requirements.

Trailers

Traditional travel trailers are the least expensive snowbird option, a new 16' model costing as low as $14,000, although the Ontario-manufactured custom-built Award and legendary Airstream brands are over $50,000.

Rear wheel drive vehicles with V-6 engines are adequate to pull trailers up to 3500 pounds, but 8 cylinders (as in a Suburban, large SUV, or pickup truck) are required for heavier units. Care must be taken in choosing the hitch to connect the two components.

Travel trailer combinations are the most **challenging** of the options to pilot, often measuring over 50 feet in length when you include the connector. The location of the hitch gives the trailer considerable leverage to push around the towing vehicle and, combined with a high profile and lightweight construction, the load can be difficult to control in strong winds and when passed by large trucks. (Sway bars, notably the Hensley Arrow, help.) Hi-Lo and TrailManor models, in which the top collapses into the bottom of the unit, are less vulnerable to wind, but the resulting shortage of cupboards is a disadvantage.

Backing a trailer into a site requires practice, patience, and good communication between driver and navigator. Unhitching and re-hitching are not fun, and drive-through campsites are usually in short supply.

There is little under-space in a standard trailer for golf clubs, fishing rods, barbecues, folding chairs, and such, although there will probably be room inside the towing vehicle and a storage pod can be added to its roof. Some new trailers have "garage" space at the back for motor-bikes, dune buggies, etc.

With functional floor plans and all the basic furnishings and appliances, many snowbirds do just fine in a regular trailer.

Fifth Wheels

A fifth wheel is a type of trailer with a raised front that hangs over the box of a pickup or "medium duty truck" and fastens onto a hitch in the truck-bed. Because of the location of the hitch directly over the rear axle of the truck, a fifth wheel has more stability, less sway, a shorter turning radius, and greater ease of handling and hitching than a standard trailer. In spite of the high profile, heavier construction materials make it less susceptible to crosswinds, and wind deflectors attached to the truck roof (less effective with a regular trailer) will further improve drivability.

Usually larger, sturdier, and better finished than trailers, "fivers" are popular with long-term snowbirds and full-timers, especially those who hunker down in one location for long periods. There is more storage space than in a trailer, although little in the truckbed because of the hitch location, and headroom in the upstairs sleeping area may be low. Again there are garage models.

A new 20' fifth wheel can be bought for as low as $20,000, but the **towing vehicle** can cost considerably more. If the rig is less than 32 feet in length you can use a regular pickup truck, but if it is longer you should have a medium duty truck conversion, which author/RVer Bill Farlow calls "a pickup on steroids". The base retail price of a new 2010 39 foot New Horizons Majestic was listed at $145,570.

Although newer trucks are quieter and more comfortable, many still find large ones cumbersome to get in and out of, to drive, and to park. We have seen fifth wheels towed by Freightliners pulling a small car, but it is not legal in many states and provinces.

A written examination and road test with an appropriate vehicle combination are needed to obtain the **Code 51 Endorsement** required on trailers over 4600 kg in British Columbia. (*Towing a Recreational Trailer*, prepared by the Insurance Corporation of B.C., is the recommended study guide.) For **air brake** licensing requirements, in B.C. contact the Motor Vehicles Branch or ICBC. Other provinces and states may have similar specifications.

Hauling a fiver will use more fuel than a lighter-weight trailer, but, factoring in a truck as the runabout vehicle, it is debatable how fuel costs compare with the motorhome/car option.

Motorized (Motorhomes)

A motorhome is less affected by crosswinds and, even with a tow vehicle, is easier to handle on the highway than a truck/fiver (/trailer) combination. It is also simpler to park.

To most, the main advantage of a motorhome is that it is **self-contained**, giving access to the fridge and washroom from the driving area without having to brave the elements, plus immediate access to the ignition if your surroundings make you uneasy. For safety reasons, walking around during travel should be avoided. (There is a story of a motorhome driver who supposedly set his vehicle on cruise control and went to make a sandwich...)

At 30' there is room for a queen-sized island bed, adequate bathroom, dinette, and sofa (26' with a chair in place of the sofa). Most motorhomes have built-in propane tanks and generators. "Toy hauler" models, with a large outside rear cargo area underneath a raised bed, can carry big boys' toys.

Class A Motorhomes

Class A's, the largest members of the motorhome family, have the greatest storage capacity, as well as grand picture windows in the cab–highly desirable in the mountains. Some models, in which a queen-sized bed is lowered from the ceiling, are as short as 24', but most new Class A's are at least 29' long, 102" wide, and equipped with a slideout, or two, or more.

Units over 40' in length are illegal in some states for travel off the interstate highways. The 102" width has also been questioned, but to my knowledge has never been formally contested. The flat front of Class A coaches has raised safety concerns. As with fifth wheel combinations, a special license endorsement is often required for units with air brakes.

Starting at around $75,000, with Class A motorhomes the sky is the limit, the ones in the upper price range built on a bus chassis, with marble or granite floors and counters, sculpted area rugs, glove leather upholstery, crystal chandeliers, Jacuzzis, Sleep Number beds, 43" TV's, massaging chairs, and perhaps a fireplace. If you are interested in such opulence you should be looking at Blue Bird, Newell, or Foretravel Motorcoaches. Or how about a Liberty Coach Elegant Lady at around $2,000,000?

Much less expensive and far more common is the ubiquitous Bounder, for many years the best selling motorhome in North America. Less costly still, Winnebago's (or Itasca's) entry level models are personally recommended.

Another option is a camperized bus, which will have a tough engine, long life, and no weight or built-in safety issues (check out busnuts.com). Our first RV was a small school bus.

Our Itasca Class A at Pahrump, Nevada

Class C Motorhomes

Until recently the Class C motorhome, built on a cutaway chassis with a van cab, was identifiable by the extension over the cockpit and was considered the smaller, poorer cousin to the Class A. Its size and style have changed–newer models up to 40' in length and often with no overhang. The onboard equipment is basically the same and decorating similar to Class A's, although C's lack the panoramic front windows, spacious driving cab, and front seats which swivel to become part of the living area. Another disadvantage for long-term RVers is limited outside storage in many models.

On the **plus side**, an extension over the cab offers protection from the sun and rain, and the driver's door is easily manageable. The smaller models are more maneuverable than large Class A's, offer more flexibility of parking, and do not require a tow vehicle, although most snowbirds have one. Also, according to the RV Consumers Group, because of the cab protrusion, Class C motorhomes are safer than Class A's. The gas mileage, at about 10 miles per Canadian gallon, is no better than a Class A of the same length as the weight is about the same.

New Class C's start as low as $50,000, but heavier safer C+ units built on a medium truck chassis are considerably more, and can go as high as $400,000+ for a Dynamax Grand Sport with a Mercedes Benz engine and Freightliner chassis. Much smaller and less expensive, but highly regarded, is the Lazy Daze brand (for which there is detailed information in Joan Taylor's articles at rversonline.org).

In small Class C's the overhang or dinette must be used for sleeping, but those over 23' usually offer a separate back corner bed, and most over 26' have an actual bedroom. Retirees often use the overhang for a built-in entertainment centre, which looks classy and solves the dilemma of where to put the television, but adds to the cost and weight of the RV and takes away storage space.

As the most popular model with **rental** companies, Class C's over three years old (usually with high mileage, but conscientious maintenance) are often for sale at large dealerships in rental hubs such as Vancouver, Calgary, and Toronto. Conversely, a newer purchase can be put into a rental program, saving the sales tax and gaining income tax advantages, maintenance and storage benefits, and possibly substantial rental income. The downside is wear and tear on the unit and increased insurance costs. If you rent out privately you must obtain a special clause on your insurance.

Our Yellowstone Class C in Oregon

Van Conversions

Van conversions, or Class B motorhomes, are geared to traveling singles or couples, the Roadtrek and Pleasure-Way brands manufactured in Canada. At 7' to 9' in height (some have pop-tops) and 17' to 22' in length, they are the most compact, fuel-efficient, and easiest to handle RV option. They also offer a greater choice of routes and campsites than larger models. A van conversion can be used for day-to-day transportation and can be parked in your driveway, although when it is gone from your house, it is obvious that you too are away.

Predictably, size is also the major drawback, particularly for large-size occupants. Although most Class B motorhomes are fully self-contained and at least 6' in interior height, living quarters are constricted. The dinette table or sofa doubles as a bed and the tiny bathroom is also the shower stall. The kitchen area is functional for little more than cereal, soup, and sandwiches. Storage is extremely limited inside and out, although a pod can be attached to the roof. Small holding tanks limit dry camping, and units under 22' are not accepted in some parks.

Although there will be no tow vehicle to worry about, you will have to disconnect the water, electricity, and sewer whenever you want to leave the campground. The choice of parking spaces when shopping and touring will be less than for a tow car.

Van conversions are the most expensive recreational vehicle per square foot, starting at about $70,000 for a new unit, more than some Class C's. Suitable for usage as every-day vehicles, insurance rates are also steep. Built on a van chassis, they have a low gross vehicle weight rating (see the next chapter).

More roomy for long-term travel is the new-on-the-scene class B+ motorhome–a cross between Class B and C.

I Go Where I'm Towed

The great majority of Class A and Class C motorhomes on snowbird highways are followed closely by a "toad" or "dinghy", a fuel-efficient towed vehicle for shopping and sightseeing. With a tow car, once hooked up to the resort's utilities the motorhome can stay put until it is time to move on.

For dinghy towing you can use a dolly (which carries two car wheels) or a trailer (which carries the whole car), but these options take extra maintenance, require license plates, and pose a storage problem at most campgrounds.

The easiest and most popular method is to tow with four wheels on the ground. This is possible for most cars with standard transmissions, but other than certain models of Saturns, the great majority of automatics are not manufacturer-approved for unrestricted towing in this manner, and warranties will be void in cases of engine or transmission damage. Some can become approved with the addition of devices such as transmission lubrication pumps, transmission uncouplers, and/or drive-wheel lockouts (see remcotowing.com). Others, like certain Honda CRVs, are sanctioned with the stipulation you run the car engine every 200 miles or so.

Each January, *MotorHome* magazine and the FMCA website give an update on approved towables and guidelines for towing. It is advisable to get approval in writing from the manufacturer before purchasing.

Prior to beginning a dinghy search check out the weight your motorhome is approved to pull (see next chapter). For gasoline-powered rigs a vehicle less than 3000 pounds is recommended. Low weight is another plus for Saturns. It's unfortunate for RVers that General Motors has discontinued the brand.

Toads require a hitch (ideally attached to the motorhome rather than the car), as well as a coordinating electrical system, and safety chains. Many, including the RV Consumers Group (rv.org), also advocate the towed vehicle have its own braking system (see next chapter), which is activated with that of the motorhome. In British Columbia a tow car whose weight is more than 2800 kilograms (6173 pounds) or more than 40% of the weight of the towing vehicle, is required by law to have such a system. Other provinces and states may have similar restrictions.

Be aware that a motorhome-dinghy combination cannot be backed up more than a few feet without damaging the car's steering system. It is imperative a Sunbelt toad have air conditioning.

Some dinghies have signs claiming:
I'M NOT BEING TOWED
I'M PUSHING

Towable or Motorized?

After all that discussion—for those of you who have never driven a truck, do you want to start now so that you can pull a fifth wheel or trailer? For those already part of the truck scene, will your present one work as a towing vehicle, or are you looking for a reason to upgrade, or to purchase a more low-profile fuel-efficient car?

There are pros and cons for both motorized and non-motorized RV's. Lifestyle, experience, and budget should be the determinants. In 2011, for environmental and financial reasons, there is a trend away from large gas-guzzling vehicles and towards light-weight trailers and smaller motorhomes.

Automotive and Structural Considerations

Once you have established whether you want a motorhome or a towable, length should be the next consideration, followed by cargo carrying capacity, and automotive and structural features. Prospective RV purchasers should check out the website of the RV Consumers Group at rv.org.

Budget should, of course, be an overriding guide in your shopping.

Size Matters

Before getting too attached to that 40' rig with washer and dryer, king-sized bed, bath and a half, and four slideouts, consider fuel costs and maneuverability, plus the greater range of campsites, roads, fuel outlets, and parking available with a smaller unit. As well, consider it is advisable both travel partners can drive the rig. And, further, remember that in many provinces and states large trucks and coaches with air brakes require special license endorsements, transgression possibly causing insurance problems in an accident.

On the other hand, be sure you have enough room to live comfortably for a lengthy period, and that you have all the furniture and storage space you will require. The ideal unit is 40' when parked and 20' on the road. Model numbers always make the RV shorter—an Itasca 27C is 27'11" in length.

Watch Your Weight

Of prime importance in any recreational vehicle is its **gross vehicle weight rating**—the maximum allowable weight of the loaded RV, information which can usually be found inside a cupboard or driver's door, as well as in sales brochures and owners' manuals. Manufacturers now give the "cargo carrying capacity", which saves computations.

In older rigs, to determine the weight you are allowed in equipment, fuel, fresh and waste water, supplies, passengers, etc., subtract the net (empty) weight of the rig from the GVWR. Check if once-nonstandard items such as awnings, generators, and air conditioners are included in the posted net weight.

It is recommended that you verify net and packed weight at a truck weigh station (sometimes free in Canada, a challenge in the U.S.). An overloaded vehicle will be difficult to handle, have inadequate power on hills, and risk damage to the suspension, brakes, and tires. Exceeding the GVWR is also illegal and subject to roadside checks.

One U.S. gallon of gas will add about 6 pounds, a gallon of diesel 7 pounds, a gallon of propane 4.2 pounds, and a gallon of water/sewage 8.3 pounds. On the metric scale one litre of liquid weighs approximately one kilogram. Be sure you have a reasonable weight allowance to work with before purchasing an RV and check the owner's manual for the gross combined weight rating (GCWR) of a motorhome before buying a tow vehicle.

Chassis

Traditionally, the majority of Class A's, on a stripped-rail chassis, were produced by Ford or Chevrolet, but a few years back Workhorse replaced the latter. Most large luxury coaches are manufactured by Roadmaster, Freightliner, or Spartan, and buses have a Prevost chassis.

J.D. Gallant's intensive study on motorhomes for the RV Consumers' Group determined that a wheelbase distance between axles of less than 54% of the overall length would present difficulty in steering, particularly in tight turns. Also a long overhang will drag in road dips.

Gas Versus Diesel

Many motorhome owners swear by or lust after diesel engines and the power they provide–necessary in large coaches and appreciated on long hills. Diesel engines get three to five miles per gallon more than gasoline-powered ones, are more reliable, require fewer repairs, have a much longer life, and offer a quieter ride in the cockpit. Any truck stop works for fueling up.

On the other hand, diesel-powered rigs cost considerably more than comparable gas-powered units, are more expensive to maintain and repair, are slow to accelerate, and are loud and smelly to the outside world. Another consideration is that most have air brakes, which require a special license endorsement. At one time cheaper, in 2011 diesel fuel costs about the same or more than gasoline. However, large fifth wheels *require* diesel-powered trucks and it is accepted that motorhomes over 35' should have diesel engines.

In 2011 manufacturers are responding to the new environmentally-conscious world with smaller lighter-weight models and more efficient fuel consumption. Some are offering hybrids.

Safety Features

All new recreational vehicles come with warning devices for smoke, carbon monoxide, and LP-gas leaks. Older models without should have them installed. Batteries must be changed periodically for the smoke and CO detectors, but the sensor for LP gas works off the house battery. Overfill protection devices are now required on propane tanks and those without will not be filled in the U.S. Older tanks can be adapted.

Alternate Power Sources

Generators, which provide a backup power source when a plug-in is not available, are now standard in Class A's and an important option in Class C's, Class B's, and towables. In motorhomes they draw fuel from the vehicle's engine and will not operate when the tank is below a certain level, to prevent stranding inattentive campers. Trailers and fifth wheels require portable units, which operate on their own propane or gas supply. Look for quiet, efficient, lightweight models, considering Honda and Yamaha brands.

Gensets are invaluable as a source of electricity when dry camping but are looked on as noisy polluters by many, and a large number of parks forbid or limit their usage. Newer models are less offensive.

Inverters also allow operation of household appliances without shore power, drawing energy from coach batteries rather than fuel and thus having no exhaust. They vary greatly in power and price—at Camping World from $40 to $3000. **Solar panels** are necessary with larger models to keep batteries charged.

Basements

Adding a foot or so in height to the 1985 Bounder allowed for large storage compartments below the floorboards. In the early "basement models" there was barely enough allowance in the GVWR, however, for passengers and gas, let alone food and golf clubs. The higher profile also meant a less streamlined appearance and greater wind deflection. But the concept caught on, manufacturers made adjustments to increase gross vehicle weight ratings and improved the styling, and now virtually all Class A motorhomes and some Class C's have basements, an important feature for long-term RVers.

Slideouts

Slideouts were the next major innovation in the RV world, almost all Class A's and fifth wheels manufactured after 2002 having at least one, as well as many Class C's, B's, trailers, and even campers on truckbeds.

Sliders undisputedly expand living space, give a more homelike, less boxcar-like feeling, and open up a greater variety of floor plans. They can be up to 42" in depth, but bigger is not always better. An 18" slide adds roominess without limiting campsites, impeding living space, or cutting off the fridge and/or bathroom when retracted.

Slideouts add to the price, weight, fuel bill, and sometimes the cost of an extended warranty. They are a drain on batteries—an important factor when dry camping. They can restrict movement inside the rig when retracted and in certain models cut off access to outside storage compartments when extended. They are one more thing that can go wrong.

There have been cases of accumulated ice preventing operation of the slider, its floor sagging in humid climates, and of units inching out while traveling, with a resulting accumulation of grit and moisture on top (which also occurs in models with no protective awning when parked). The overall strength of the rig is lessened by the holes cut in the frame to accommodate the slides, and in some models movement of the driver's seat is restricted. Construction has improved over the years.

In spite of their negative features, slideouts are here to stay, the great majority of RVers wanting them. When looking for a rig in 2004, we declared we didn't need slideouts, but got a unit with two 18" ones and were delighted with the extra space.

Important considerations—sliders on the "neighbour side" do not infringe on "your" outside living space or limit your awning extension, and slideouts on both sides can make a tight campsite really cramped.

Toy Haulers

The most recent addendum is "garage" space at the rear of both motorized and non-motorized RV's, often with hydraulic lifts to load in boats, dune buggies, motorcycles, motorized golf carts, etc. Keep in mind the extra weight in carrying these "toys" and that their fuel tanks may be a safety risk.

Levelers

To keep your fridge happy, your rig must be parked level. Hydraulic levelers, once an expensive luxury, are now standard in Class A motorhomes, although two by fours and/or Lynx blocks should still be used on soft ground and hot asphalt. Trailers and fifth wheels need stabilizing jacks. Electric levelers are available for fivers.

Rear View Systems

Another expensive option, now the norm in Class A motorhomes, rear vision (back-up) systems, consisting of a camera on the exterior and a monitor on the dashboard, are invaluable in parking and good for keeping tabs on a towed vehicle on the highway. Because of their smaller dashboard, installation is not always possible on Class

C's. The outside camera of some models is easy to steal—we learned through personal experience.

Of course trailers need adequate side mirrors.

Auxiliary Braking Systems

In response to manufacturers' recommendations and state and provincial laws, as well as for peace of mind on mountain roads, an increasing number of motorhome drivers are purchasing auxiliary braking devices. Systems such as U.S. Gear and Brake Buddy activate the brakes on the towed vehicle when those on the motorhome are applied. According to RV tech expert Bob Livingston, diesel pushers can handle heavier dinghy vehicles without extra brakes.

All towables but the lightest-weight trailers should have their own supplementary brake controls.

Roofs

Winnebago promotes its fiberglass roof as more attractive, durable, and cleaner than rubber, and claims to all but eliminate the dreaded black streak problem common with aluminum roofs and to a lesser extent with rubber. Experts say a fiberglass top requires more maintenance, however, to prevent it from becoming porous. A ladder for roof access is standard on most rigs.

Brands

Quality varies greatly from manufacturer to manufacturer, the best resource being J.D. Gallant's *RV Ratings Guide*, published as a book from 1990 to 2003, at which time the series was replaced by *RV Ratings CD-ROM*, available through the rv.org website. Research thoroughly and be aware that if a manufacturer goes out of business, its warranties are no longer valid.

The **dealership** should also be a major consideration in choosing an RV, for follow-up with problems which will inevitably develop. You want one fairly close to home with a large service department and a good reputation. Check with the Better Business Bureau.

The Livability Factor

With some RV's you do an about-turn at the door. Others warrant going inside. Then there's the one where it's love at first sight.

Do a "mock live-in" with a unit you have bonded with: lie on the bed, sit on the toilet, get in the shower, analyze storage space. Check out the GVWR and do a body and cursory mechanical inspection. (A thorough examination by a licensed technician is needed before you make a definite commitment.) If you like what you see, with a motorhome take a test drive and discuss the pros and cons thoroughly–offsite.

If you still love it, with a motorhome consider renting the unit, or similar one, for a short trip, so you can check out the electrical, heating, and water systems, as well as the appliances and overall livability. Again, because of complexity coordinating with a towing vehicle, specific rental trailers can be difficult to find.

Entries

Entry doors in front of the passenger seat in diesel coaches where there is no engine hump, and at the back in some trailers, free up the rest of the interior for usable living space. However, a door in the middle of the unit, although always narrow, is more convenient when loading and unloading, barbecuing, or dining outside. Screen doors are important for ventilation and communication.

Those with arthritis will find some entry steps difficult, the ones on motorhomes usually lower than on trailers and fifth wheels, which often require a portable platform step. Grab bars are standard at entries, but vary in helpfulness.

Driver doors in motorhomes are handy when getting fuel, and help conserve the carpet in the living area, but because of their height off the ground are often unused in Class A's. Those in Class C's are much lower.

Bedroom

Sleeping accommodations are of great importance to long-term RVers–convertible dinette tables not ideal. A corner bed (with adjacent bathroom) is good for afternoon naps but somewhat snug for two bulky adults all night. Also consider bathroom trips and making the bed.

A separate bedroom is desirable, and accessibility makes island and twin beds preferable to one against a wall. Queen-sized units vary in dimensions from rig to rig and are usually smaller than their residential counterparts. A piece of foam will counteract the typically firm RV mattress.

Is there a storage area under the bed? Do struts make it easy to use? Is there enough drawer and closet space? Are the lamps adequate for reading? Is there a TV outlet? Are there night tables, or at least a drawer between twin beds for glasses, books, tissues, etc.? Has the fifth wheel bedroom adequate headroom and easy stairs?

Bathroom

Author/RV salesman Don Wright claims that veteran RVers consistently rank bathroom size, location, layout, and features among the most important considerations in the purchase of a new unit. A split bathroom gives extra dressing space, but the toilet stall is often tight, some, according to Mr. Wright, "suitable to do your business, but you have to step into the hall to do the paperwork".

Is the toilet seat high enough? (Most new rigs have higher ones.) Is the shower large enough? Is a bathtub necessary? (Useful for dirty doggie feet.) Is there adequate room for toiletries and towels? Is there a window and/or a vent? Is there space for a waste basket?

Kitchen

Do you require a conventional oven? Many newer models have only a microwave/convection combination. Is there room to stand in front of the oven door to remove a turkey, or at least a pizza?

Do you need an icemaker? (Portable ones are available.) A three-way fridge can be kept on during travel, but as long as the unit is cold when you start out and the door not opened several times, there should be no problem turning it off for a few hours. (Sometimes when stopped for lunch we put ours on propane-mode).

Is the counter space workable? There will never seem like enough, but the stove and sink(s) can be covered, and if there isn't a fold-up extension at the end of the counter probably one can be added. Is there room for a small garbage receptacle (ideally under the sink)?

Are there sufficient cupboards and drawers and do they latch well? (Light-weight items can be stored in the oven and/or microwave if necessary.) Slide-out pantry shelves are handy. Granite counters are impressive, but add a lot of weight and dollars.

Don't look for a dishwasher unless you are considering a new high-end coach. Although requiring a 50 amp plug-in and considerable space, they will no doubt become more common, but in the mean-time the vast majority of RVers "rough it" and wash by hand.

New on the scene are outdoor kitchens—large compartments with a fridge, grill, and cupboards.

Dining Area

Free-standing tables and chairs look more classy, but you lose the storage space and additional bed offered with bench models, plus extra chairs require storage. Drawers under bench seats make retrieval of items easier. Is the dinette seating comfortable? (Especially important in units without a sofa.)

Living "Room"

Are the reading lights and television in suitable locations? Also, is the TV in a *safe* location, and is it a digital model? Is the seating comfortable? Is there a place to park your coffee or martini? If not, TV trays work (wooden ones look better). In motorhomes a steering wheel table (attaches on), with a cover and perhaps a lamp, gives the area a homey appearance. Recliners and bucket chairs are popular. Some rigs have fireplaces.

I question the taste of some RV decorators, particularly regarding fabric and the overuse of mirrors, which on walls and doors make the rig appear larger—but on the backsplash in the kitchen area? Personal items, an attractive table centerpiece, rugs, and cushions can make the most basic RV appealing.

Computer Area

Large fifth wheels usually have a built-in computer area and some Class A's have a pullout workstation in front of the passenger seat. As most RVers have laptops, a small fold-down table in the living area or the dinette table works just fine. Camping World does offer special computer tables.

Windows

Windows are important for light, fresh air, and bringing the outside in when parked on the Gulf of Mexico or Sonoran Desert, but in a smaller RV the view will be at the expense of cupboards. Dual-pane windows help keep heat and noise in or out, and limit condensation in colder locations. Jalousie windows (with slats) are preferable to sliding ones, for security and protection from driving rain.

Day/night shades let daylight in and help keep drafts out while maintaining privacy. But beware—the "day" part is transparent at night with lights on, as a friend of ours discovered while cooling off in her birthday suit one evening. (Her horrified husband was outside the rig shooting the bull with the guys!)

Keeping Cool

As shade trees are few and far between in most snowbird parks, without an overhang it is usually too hot to sit outside in the daytime. An **awning** also extends your living area into the outdoors, offers protection from rain, and helps cool the inside of the rig as well as a curbside refrigerator. Protective canopies are now included over slideouts, and many RV's have them over doors and windows.

Basic awnings are a chore to put up and down and a hazard in the wind, but for $2000 or so you can get one with push button controls and a sensor for automatic retraction in sustained winds. However, with automatic controls you can't slant the canvas for rain run-off or secure it to the ground.

An **air conditioner** is a necessity in the Sunbelt and now standard in Class A motorhomes. Many snowbird rigs have two, but often one is replaced with a thermostatically-controlled **Fan-Tastic Fan/Vent,** which is more energy-efficient and can operate off the RV battery—ideal for leaving a pet unattended in the rig for short periods when not plugged in. The "Magic Fan" can be complemented by a roof cover so you can keep its vent open while traveling, and also with rain sensors for automatic closure, although the closing and re-opening can be annoying at night. Remote control kits are available.

Small Ticket Items

Although not installable in all rigs, an exterior **LP gas outlet** eliminates the need for bulky propane tanks for the barbecue. Some newer RV's have grilling racks on the outside connected to an interior propane source. A **water filtration system** will remove some impurities and improve the taste of local and chlorinated water, although will not make Mexican water drinkable. A dealership will usually throw in a DVD player and/or bedroom TV.

Not Necessary

Onboard **washers and dryers** add extra weight, use fuel, and take up valuable space. Also they require 50 amp power which costs extra at most RV parks, are limited in load capacity, are prone to wrinkling, and will deprive you of laundry room socialization. Many RVers would not be without them, but others have existing units removed.

Stick model **vacuum cleaners** work just fine and are less cumbersome than a built-in system. A broom and dustpan are necessary with both.

Built-in **satellite dishes** are easier but portable ones are much less pricey.

Special Needs

Several RV manufacturers, notably Winnebago, build specially equipped units or adapt standard models to meet individual needs. Lifts can be installed, aisles widened, bathrooms customized, handrails and custom cabinets mounted, light switches and thermostats lowered. Hand controls can be put in the driving cab.

The perfect rig does not exist. The aim is to find one which comes close to meeting your needs and budget and personalizing it.

Making the Deal

As you gaze in horror at the bottom line on the spec sheet, realize that there is always considerable wiggle room on the manufacturer's suggested retail price. Especially in a weak economy.

Wheeling and Dealing

Dealers as a rule pay 30 to 35% less than the MSRP and will often take a small profit on a sale, with the expectation of making money later servicing the RV. With new units ask to see the dealer's invoice and do not pay more than 80% of the suggested retail price. For new U.S.-made rigs the Canadian price will always reflect the exchange rate.

A **trade-in** affects the discount. The more you are given for your old RV, the less the markdown on the new one, but with a trade you will pay tax only on the difference between the two units.

It is in the **off-season** that you will be able to negotiate the best price, December and January being prime RV purchase months. My sister got an exceptional deal on a Winnebago Sightseer on December 18 with a dealership which wanted the unit off its books before year-end. The almost identical Itasca Sunova promoted by the **competition** helped the bargaining process. **Month-end** is also a good time to buy, when dealers or salesmen are trying to sell "just one more" to reach quotas or gain bonuses.

If it seems you have reached an impasse on price negotiations, often a sales manager will include equipment such as a Fan-Tastic Fan, water filtration system, and/or propane barbecue connection, which you probably intended to purchase anyway.

Out-of-Country Purchases

With the vast selection and low prices south of the border, it is tempting to buy an RV in the United States, but because of hassles with emission testing, vehicle inspections, and possible modifications required to meet Canadian standards, transborder purchases should be carefully thought through. We heard of a man whose rig bought in the U.S. was refused licensing in Canada without costly alterations. He ended up selling it back in the States at a substantial loss.

Consider the exchange rate, that there may be difficulty getting financing for a U.S.-purchased unit, and that it is good to be near your dealership.

If you are seriously considering a cross-border purchase, call the Federal Department of Transportation (800 511-7755) and the Registrar of Imported Vehicles for Canada (888 848-8240) to check that your chosen RV can be imported, and get the fax number for vehicle registration. With free trade there are no import duties and there will be no U.S. taxes, but you are responsible for an administration charge (about $200) plus GST and PST (HST) on the price before trade-in.

Insurance must be arranged ahead of time and you are required to contact the customs office at the point of entry at least 72 hours prior to crossing, when you will need the certificate of title, bill of sale, and proof of vehicle registration in Canada. You then have 45 days to complete required modifications and to get provincial license plates.

The Pre-owned RV

The pristine condition, attached warranties, and decorating options of a factory-direct recreational vehicle are appealing, but not financially feasible for many. It is reported two out of three purchasers buy a used unit and about the same number obtain financing, although the latter statistic is probably lower for retirees.

On the other hand, it is easier to get a good deal on a "mature" unit as a motorized RV loses 30% of the MSRP as soon as it is driven off the lot, a further 10-15% after the first year, and about 6% each subsequent year. Towables retain their value better. The ideal pre-owned RV is two to three years old, with low mileage and the kinks worked out, but these are hard to find as the average RVer keeps his rig about five years.

Be aware that some RV resorts will not accept units over 10 years of age and that RV appliances, whose life expectancy is about a decade, are expensive to replace. Also, for recreational vehicles which are no longer manufactured it may be difficult or impossible to get parts, and warranties no longer apply. The number of "orphan" RV's has increased greatly during the recent recession.

You can likely negotiate a better price with a **private sale** than at a dealership and will save sales tax, although an owner who purchased when the exchange rate was less attractive may have an unrealistic view on his rig's value. There are always units advertised in newspapers, RV publications, and on the Internet, but in the latter case many are from dealers looking for leads. Keep in mind that if you purchase privately you will have no recourse with undetected problems and you may have to worry about selling your present RV.

An inspection by a qualified technician is especially important with a private sale. The Recreation Dealers Association of Canada has created a Pre-Owned Certified Inspection Program, whose report could help a private seller, as well as the purchaser.

A business with a reputation to protect will usually repair and stand behind existing problems in a used unit, although you should still get a detailed inspection report. Traveland in Langley, B.C. paid over $1000 for the repair of the ABS brake system on our used Yellowstone two weeks after purchase. Dealing with a company also makes it easy to obtain financing and an extended warranty, although the latter is sometimes available for private sales through dealerships and insurance companies.

Beware of **consignment sales**, where the dealer will not put money into a unit before a firm sale. Satisfaction is more likely where the business owns the rig outright. One consignment lot owner offered to draw up the paperwork so we could deal directly with the owner and save the federal tax. It didn't sound quite right.

We were also understandably leery of an entrepreneur in Calgary who bought RV's in compassionate situations down south and drove them back to Canada to sell. With private sales and small companies be cautious, in the latter case contacting the Better Business Bureau.

As price guides for used U.S. brands, consult the *Kelley Blue Book* or *NADA Consumer Vehicle Appraisal Guide,* available at most large RV dealerships, banks, and libraries. Unfortunately there is no *Lemon Aid Guide* for recreational vehicles but there are reference guides by J.D. Gallant and the JR Consumer Resources group, as well as the nadaguides.com and rv.org websites.

For Canadian brands contact the Canadian Automobile Association for values and consumer reports, research classified ads, talk to owners, and comparison shop. The purchase price should be adjusted to allow for required repairs and replacements.

You Can't Judge a Rig by its Cover

In a used RV carefully examine the roof, ceiling, vents, windows, paneling, and inside cupboards for evidence of water damage, realizing that even if a leak has been repaired the resulting mould may continue to grow. A new roof can cost over $5000.

A musty smell can indicate a leak problem, or a smoker. The only questions asked by a sales manager regarding our prospective trade-in were, "Does it leak, and has it been smoked in?" Apparently the two major considerations in a used unit. (Another salesperson asked about the condition of the upholstery.) Most of today's RV owners do not smoke in their rigs but it was not always that way.

Scrutinize fiberglass siding for bulging or separation and aluminum for pitting. Look for signs of body damage, and examine the undercarriage for rust and/or salt, indicators that suspension components may fail prematurely. Wear on the inside of tires can mean alignment problems. Check for floor irregularities and uneven counters.

Inspect electrical, water, sewage, and propane systems, and monitor panels, for problems, features, and methods of operation. Turn on the air conditioner, the microwave, generator, water heater, furnace, fridge, stove burners, and lights. Rust in the water heating compartment may indicate the heater needs to be replaced. Make sure the toilet bowl will hold water, as installation of a new ring is costly.

As discussed in a previous chapter, analyze the structural and design features and especially the GVWR. Look for smoke and propane detectors and for RVIA, CSA, and CRVA stickers, which indicate the vehicle meets government and industry standards. Also check for good housekeeping (lift the top stove panel). If you are mechanically challenged, take along a knowledgeable friend for an inspection of the engine. Dark or burnt transmission fluid can indicate a serious problem.

With towable units check the entry doors, springs, and trailer tongue or fifth wheel king pin. The rear of a trailer should not droop. Also, determine if your tow vehicle is powerful enough for mountain hauling.

If you feel good about the unit after the visual examination, with a motorhome take it for a drive—on the highway, up and down hills, and around corners. It is often difficult to test drive a trailer or fifth wheel because of complexities of hitching, but in this case there is no engine to worry about. If you are still enthusiastic, make an appointment with a certified RV technician (not just a regular mechanic) for a complete inspection.

In private sales verify the vehicle identification number against liens or stolen property and ask for maintenance records. In B.C. (and probably other provinces) the VIN will also give a vehicle's accident history (also valuable when considering a used tow vehicle). Do not be impressed if the owner tells you the unit has been in storage for years. Rubber deteriorates, fan belts dry out, and batteries die.

When You're Sure You Want It

Do not rush into a deal. Research, compute, comparison shop, and on a used unit get a thorough inspection. If you are not in a hurry, with a new unit you can custom order upholstery, floor coverings, cabinetry, appliances, almost anything. On the other hand, with a one-of-a-kind rig which is "just right", don't let it get away.

Before signing on the dotted line, be aware that the cost of RV ownership also involves taxes, licenses, insurance, regular maintenance, repairs, camping fees, fuel, and perhaps storage costs. The jury is out on the value of an **extended warranty,** but experts say one from the manufacturer is best, and you should get a list of "exclusionary" items (which are *not* covered) in your policy, rather than those included. To quote RVer/author Bill Farlow: "The purchase of an RV is just the starter kit."

Prior to driving away get a final instructional walk-through (including how to manually retract the slideouts), and all relevant manuals. Then do a shakedown trip or two where you try out all the bells and whistles, within easy striking distance of your dealership or service center. Every RVer has a horror story of their first night–usually involving taps and hoses!

TAKING CARE OF BUSINESS

Before taking flight as an RV snowbird there are seemingly endless preparations regarding insurance, finances, communications, your home, your route, your pet, and yourself. The rig is covered in the next chapter.

Health Insurance

As provincial governments cover only a small part of the cost of out-of-country health care, a Canadian traveler without supplementary insurance risks financial disaster from a medical emergency south of the border. The BCAA cites an example of a 55 year-old man whose bill for hospitalization in California after a heart attack was $310,000.

The **Canadian Snowbird Association** has filed suits against the Ontario and B.C. governments, claiming that the amounts they pay for out-of-country care do not meet the "portability requirement" of the Canada Health Act and that snowbirds are being treated unjustly. Some headway has been made but there is still a long way to go.

Supplementary health insurance plans vary greatly in features, restrictions, and cost. Some totally disallow pre-existing conditions, some consider a symptom-free stabilization period, and others penalize a change in medication. Withholding a health condition, change in medication, or illness prior to traveling may invalidate a claim. A pre-trip medical is advised as an undiagnosed ailment could also result in rejection.

The high cost of out-of-country insurance often results in shorter snowbird vacations. Some choose an annual plan which offers an unlimited number of trips of specified length, the price difference between a 60-day **multi-trip plan** and a 120-day single trip policy usually more than the cost of a flight home. However, if you become ill in the first part of your getaway or while at home, the insurance may not cover you on a return trip. Some travelers choose a higher deductible in favour of a lower premium.

Many retirees have **pension plans** which include supplementary health coverage, but as these have a lifetime cap on benefits, some defer their usage until other plans become too expensive, and others add additional coverage, considering the capped amount too low. Increased or extended coverage with the original insurer is usually expensive and a top-up with another company is often not permitted or recommended because of possible incompatibility between the two parties. On the other hand, you may want to use your group plan to cover a high deductible, which will lower the premium on a new plan. Speak to your pension benefits representative to determine the best course of action.

Credit card companies offering out-of-country insurance have narrow restrictions on age, health, and number of days. Note that with multiple gold cards, coverage for each begins the day you leave. You cannot use 30 days from one and 30 days from another to attain 60 days coverage. Sometimes credit cards are used in conjunction with top-up insurance for extra time, but again problems can arise when you are dealing with two insurers. After considering the pros and cons, most travelers opt to have one plan for the entire time away.

Check out several companies, the Canadian Snowbird Association, Canadian Association of Retired Persons, Canadian Automobile Association, and Good Sam RV Club offering plans for members. Read the policy carefully, looking for clauses regarding transportation of family, coverage of air ambulance home, family and medical escorts, return of vehicle (including RV), and return of remains, in addition to medical costs. Consider the worst case scenario. Get an explanation of points which are unclear.

To qualify for supplementary health coverage you must make regular **provincial health care** payments, eligibility for which can be a problem for full-time RVers (discussed in a later chapter). In B.C. residents are expected to inform the Medical Services Plan if they will be out of Canada more than 60 days. Other provinces may have similar requirements.

It is important that you always carry your out-of-country insurance policy number and information when away, as well as your provincial health care card. Except in cases where immediate care is necessary, you are required to use the phone number provided, for referral to a medical facility with whom the insurer has a contract. Failure to do so may invalidate coverage.

On the bright side, supplementary insurance costs can be claimed as a medical expense at income tax time.

Vehicle Insurance

Be sure you have adequate **liability and collision** insurance on towed and towing vehicles, and that you will be covered while out of the country for a lengthy period. A few extra dollars will give protection against an uninsured driver. Vehicle contents are covered by your home insurance policy. A reduced rate will be available for long periods your rig is not on the road.

Good coverage for **emergency road service** is also important, so that you do not get stranded in the middle of nowhere as we did with our AAA Plus insurance which did not cover our Bounder. We could have saved much anguish and money had we realized we needed AAA RV Plus.

Mexican vehicle insurance, usually purchased at companies near the Mexican border (but also available at certain Canadian and U.S. outlets), is mandatory for travel into that country, to keep you out of jail in an accident, in which case all parties are routinely incarcerated until a settlement is reached. In British Columbia ICBC will reimburse part of your provincial insurance payment if you are in Mexico over 30 days. Travelers to Mexico from other provinces should check with their insurance companies.

Renewals, Finances, Mail, Etc.

Attend to anything which will come up for **renewal** during your absence, such as investment certificates, insurance policies, passports, or drivers' licenses (which can be renewed up to 180 days in advance). With expiring credit cards, arrange to have a new card sent to you down south, or be prepared to fall back on other cards or cash. Inform companies who post automatic billings to your credit card of a new number and expiration date, as payments will not be processed on an expired card.

You must also deal with automatic billings if your card company changes your account number when they think your card may have been compromised in some way. Don't forget about annual payments. I was recently informed my yearly BCAA vehicle insurance payment had been declined by MasterCard, because I had not informed BCAA of my new account information. Not good if you are away for four months.

Arrange for **direct deposit** of pensions and/or investment revenues. Obtain post-dated cheques for any private rental or loan income for the bank to post on the appropriate dates. Set up **pre-authorized bank payments** for utilities, taxes, strata fees, insurance policies, etc. Make arrangements for installment payments on income tax and transactions regarding RRSP's or RRIF's.

Credit card payments can be made by telephone banking or on-line. Alternatively, you can get monthly balances online or by phone, and mail cheques along with photocopied payment slips.

It is easier to pay just one credit card bill, but you should carry an alternate for backup. We found ourselves financially disabled one year when delayed by weather conditions after the expiry of our sole card. It is recommended you let your card company know of your travels, as in recent years a number of out-of-country transactions have been declined for security reasons.

You can arrange to have Canada Post hold or forward your **mail**– either to you if you are staying in one location, or to a relative or friend. There are also mail-forwarding services with businesses such as the UPS Store and FedEx Office, and organizations such as Good Sam and Escapees. Otherwise, enlist someone you trust to pick it up and inform you of important items.

You will have no difficulty finding **ATM** machines in the Sunbelt (I have seen them in McDonald's), but be prepared to pay several dollars for each transaction and to be puzzled by the account balance on the printout. (Is it in U.S. dollars or Canadian? How up-to-date is it?) Some bank machines have been known to issue withdrawal receipts but no cash. Best to use one at an actual bank location, rather than in a store or a strip mall. Better yet, ask for **cash back** when using your debit card at major chain stores or grocery outlets. It is recommended you carry an extra bank card in case the electronic strip on the original malfunctions. Merchants no longer like travelers' cheques.

If you are planning to roost in one spot for the winter you may want to open a **bank account** in your winter home, the Canadian Snowbird Association offering a currency exchange program for automatic transfers into a U.S. account, at a preferred exchange rate, with no transfer fees. Foreign exchange outlets usually offer better rates than banks for changing money before leaving home.

Leave behind a will, ideally with a lawyer.

Keeping in Touch

Wireless phones have taken over the world, including the snowbird community. At one time considered too expensive for everyday usage on the road, telephone companies now offer attractive international plans, although some RVers make do with their home plan, keeping the cellular phone for emergencies or perhaps turning it on for a couple of hours each evening. (A cellphone with no affiliation can be used to access 911 as long as it is charged.) Reception is often a problem, but can be improved with a larger external antenna, power booster or amplifier, or repeater system (expensive). A recent survey by author/RVer Peggi McDonald found the most popular cellphone systems with snowbirds were TracFone and Net 10, both available at Walmart.

An expensive BlackBerry or iPhone is probably more than you need, especially if you travel with a computer. Also available south of the border, if you can give a U.S. address, are disposable phones with inexpensive calling.

With virtually all RV parks now Internet-friendly, a growing number of snowbirds use **electronic mail** to keep in touch. With an Internet server (such as Shaw, Telus, or Hotmail), a personal e-mail address, and a password, one can use e-mail anywhere there is a computer and reception. *Trailer Life* and *Woodall's* guides describe wi-fi service (and fees) at each of their listings. Although expensive, some RVers purchase USB modems for independent Internet access.

As a safety measure to get drivers off the road more frequently, an increasing number of interstate rest areas offer free wireless fidelity reception. Check out wififreespot.com for locations (including campgrounds) with service at no cost, but for sensitive transactions, like banking or bill paying, use a wireless card in free public hotspots.

Many use social networking sites like Twitter or Facebook and often enhance their Internet travel journals with photographs (from a digital camera). More and more are using **Skype**, a program with free Internet download, which converts computers to telephones–to other Skype members' computers for free, or to a landline or mobile phone for about 2 cents a minute. With a webcam added to the headset required for the audio, you can also get video.

Pocketmail, a mini-computer on which you compose a message (with limited text), dial a toll-free number, and then hold the device up to a phone receiver to send e-mail, once a staple of long-term RVers, has gone out of business.

Although cellular products are less expensive in the United States, you may wish to allow time before your departure to try out new devices and compare service plans. You may also want to check out satellite TV options for Canadian reception, Shaw Direct (previously Star Choice) preferable to ExpressVu, which does not sanction Canadian channels south of the border.

Even technologically-savvy RVers, especially those without an international cellphone plan, should have a telephone **calling card**, AT&T and Telus offering snowbird options. Be sure to use the toll-free access number to avoid costly charges by U.S. phone companies.

For calls *within* the States, going through the Canadian operator is expensive, as we found with a $7.40 Telus billing for a one minute call within Utah. A prepaid U.S. phone card would be much less costly. In Mexico purchase a Ladatel card after entering the country.

With the wireless phone era, public telephones are hard to find, those generating little revenue removed and few new ones installed.

Some RV parks now offer phone service only at individual sites (for a fee, no public phone), so consider packing your own plug-in model.

Message retrieval from your home answering machine is another way to keep in touch. Be sure to leave an emergency number with a neighbor.

Preparing Your Home

If you regularly park the RV in the driveway, it is a good idea to put it in storage for a month or two prior to leaving, so that you do not announce your departure to would-be burglars.

Windows should have good **locks**, exterior doors should have at least a one-inch deadbolt, sliding windows or doors should have a metal or wooden rod on the track, and ideally door hinges should be on the inside.

Clock **timers** should be used to activate lights, radios, and/or TV's. **Blinds** and curtains should not all be closed, but valuable items should be moved out of sight, and the person checking your home should change the position of the window coverings from time to time. A security **alarm system** will give peace of mind and if it is centrally monitored a reduction on your house insurance.

It is recommended travelers make an inventory of major possessions (with as many receipts as possible), take pictures or videos of rooms and belongings to support a possible insurance claim, engrave valuable items with a special marker for identification, and put jewelry and important papers in a safety deposit box.

Plan to unplug electrical **appliances** (except the fridge), to turn off pilot lights, and to drain and turn off the water system. Also to turn down the ringer on the telephone and perhaps change the message on the answering machine, but do not mention your travel plans. Learn to retrieve phone messages from afar. A radio turned to a talk show station will give the impression someone is home.

Contact your house insurer before you leave, and abide by their requirements, which will probably include having someone enter the premises every few days. If you do not live in a townhouse or condo you must arrange to have someone shovel snow and dispose of flyers or newspapers, which often arrive even after you have cancelled delivery.

Some snowbirds have a person stay in their home while they are down south, and in B.C. waterfront communities they sometimes even collect rent. Although not up to Arizona standards weather-wise, southern B.C. winters are attractive to prairie folk looking for an inexpensive getaway. House-sitting agencies are available if necessary. Check references carefully.

Don't forget to clean out the **fridge** and make arrangements for **plants**.

You and Fido

Make a trip to your doctor, dentist, and hairdresser, allowing time for follow-up appointments with the first two. Get **medication** required for the full time you are away if possible (some provinces have a 30-day limit). If your trip is longer than your allowance, be forewarned that, according to the Canadian Snowbird Association:

> *It has become almost impossible to have medication shipped over the border and U.S pharmacies will not honour a Canadian prescription. The alternative? Visiting a U.S. doctor (which can cost anywhere up to $100 just to walk through the door) to get a scrip for your medication, and then purchasing it. If you're lucky, your provincial program will reimburse you for this purchase–many will not.*

The CSA is lobbying provincial governments to allow travelers to purchase medication for their full time out of the country.

Take your pet to the groomer and to the veterinarian for a checkup and shots. We also got a letter from our vet explaining the 4 months worth of insulin we were carrying for Simba.

Planning the Trip

Poring over maps and guidebooks before you leave is half the fun. If you are not already an **AAA** member, now is the time—for the free guides, maps, and Triptiks, as well as discounts on route, and emergency road service. AAA guidebooks give detailed descriptions of cities and tourist attractions, but their campground guides should be supplemented with a *Woodall's* or *Trailer Life* version. (A survey done by rversonline.org found the latter, which gives GPS co-ordinates for listings, was more widely used.)

Consider joining the **Good Sam Club** and either **Passport America** or **Camp Club USA** for campground savings along the highway. Copy pertinent information from books and the Internet, and perhaps send for literature and discount booklets for places you plan to visit. Accordion folders are ideal for filing such items, as well as pamphlets and papers you gather on your travels.

Be sure your maps are up-to-date. Houston's ring road (which cost us over $30 in tolls each direction but saved us from downtown!) was not on our 10-year-old map of the city. The freetrip.com website is valuable for route information.

The **Rand McNally Road Atlas**, showing detailed maps, exits, counties (for weather advisories), and a plethora of travel information, including state phone numbers and websites for road conditions and construction, is an excellent resource. (The cheaper Walmart version also indicates store locations which allow overnighting.) New in 2011 is the **Trailer Life Directory RV Road Atlas**. Many RVers have **global positioning systems**.

The Next Exit (again, available at some Walmarts for cheaper than elsewhere) is also highly recommended for travel on interstate highways. And new on the scene is **Exit Now Interstate Exit Directory**, which includes everything from dangerous left exits, to dump stations, to pet hospitals, plus seemingly anything else pertinent to RVers.

Most snowbirds like to leave before the snow flies, and plan to be back in time to do income tax. Be aware that if you are in the United States more than an average of four months a year you are required to submit a waiver form to the IRS showing that you have a "closer connection" to Canada. For further details see the section on full-timing and the Revenue Canada pamphlet *Heading South*, or contact the Canadian Snowbird Association.

Many RVers prefer secondary highways to freeways, but on their initial trip south most snowbirds take Interstates 5, 15, 29/35, 75, or 95. When planning your itinerary, limit your highway time, especially if there is only one driver, and plan a break every couple of hours. The majority of RV snowbirds are on the road by seven and stop for the day just after noon.

Draw up a tentative **schedule** for those back home, but be prepared to be flexible, adapting to weather and road conditions and allowing time for detours and sidetrips. Snowbirds usually have lots of time to check out the Walmarts and wait out the storms.

GETTING READY TO ROLL

As previously mentioned, with a new rig you should take at least one trip to discover problems before venturing too far from your dealership and/or trusted mechanic. Rookie RVers can use this opportunity to practice setting up and breaking camp, particularly the dumping procedure. Check out all the systems, first with hookups and then without. Refine your backing-in routine, without a rearview monitor using hand signals or walkie talkies with your co-pilot rather than trying to communicate over engine noise.

If you have never driven anything larger than a mini-van consider instruction from a company such as Euro-Driving School near Vancouver (604 585-3876) or similar outfit specializing in big rigs (usually trucks). Okanagan University College in Kelowna offers driver training exclusively for RVers (250 862-5457), as does the RV Driving School LLC (formerly Dick Reed's) with several locations in Sunbelt America (530 878-0111 or rvschool.com). As well, most large RV dealerships can recommend a qualified instructor. Many think special training for RVers should be mandatory.

Preparing the Rig

Before tackling the interstates it is imperative your vehicles have been recently serviced and are in top mechanical condition. A tire blowout on an LA freeway or air conditioning failure in Death Valley would be unfortunate. Also have **potential problems** tended to as on-the-road breakdowns are expensive and repair work is difficult to follow up on miles down the highway. Letters in RV publications indicate that misdiagnoses and faulty workmanship are common.

When unforeseen problems arise, large national service centers are best for follow-up, but unless there is a dealership for your particular RV brand or a Camping World in the vicinity, you may have trouble finding a suitable repair facility at all. Many are not large enough to handle RV's, and truck service centers often don't want to be bothered with them, especially if there is an insurance company involved. Flying J, Pilot, TA, and Love's (the major RV fuel outlets) do not do major repair work.

Be sure you have good wiper blades and tires, a basic tool kit, a tire gauge, extra oil and other fluids, and spare filters, bulbs, belts, and fuses. An **air compressor**, which works on DC power, will allow you to tend to a low tire anywhere. (Service stations with working air pumps are few and far between.) A **battery charger** is also a good idea. Carry flares or fluorescent triangles to set out in an emergency situation. Chains for the northern leg of your trip are also recommended.

Equipping the Rig

There are countless possible accessories for your home on wheels, most found at Camping World (with locations strategically placed along or near interstates on the outskirts of major U.S. cities) and many also available at your local RV dealership. The majority of the less technical items can be found at Walmart–for a much lower price. While many gadgets are a matter of personal taste, others are necessities.

Safety Equipment

Standard in new RV's, be sure you have a **fire extinguisher**, know how to use it, and keep it charged. The rig should also have propane and smoke **detectors**. (Be sure the plastic wrappers are off the batteries.) If the smoke alarm sounds each time you make toast you can cover the sensor with a plastic bag, but don't forget to remove it when you finish cooking.

Umbilical Cords and Accessories

The rig most likely comes with a **freshwater hose,** but extra lengths should be available for a water outlet at the back of a campsite. Do not use a regular garden hose, which is not insulated and can breed bacteria, and never use the freshwater hose to rinse out the sewer hose. Connecting the hose ends when storing will help protect them from dirt and bacteria, and spraying the campground tap with a bleach solution before attachment is a further precaution.

A water **pressure regulator**, which fits between the hose and the campground tap, will protect the plumbing system from sudden surges, but can cause pressure problems in the shower. (If you have trouble rinsing out shampoo, switch to the water pump temporarily.)

Extra 10' and 20' lengths of **sewer hose** are also advised. Connectors are needed for each end of the hose and rubber sewer rings (donuts), to prevent back-up, are required by law in many states. A hose support (Slunky, Telescoper, or a piece of plastic pipe) will provide a slope for efficient drainage. Ideally, disposable gloves and paper towels should be used when dumping.

Chemicals are needed for the holding tanks to break down wastes and control odours, but those containing formaldehyde are forbidden in many states, often under penalty of a fine or expulsion from a park. As regular cleaning products can damage an RV's plumbing system, cleaner residue should be wiped out with a paper towel rather than washed down the sink.

A heavy-duty 25' **extension cord** and testing devices for voltage level and polarity of campground electricity are recommended, as are power cord adaptors, with which a 30 amp cord can be plugged into a 15 amp plug, a 50 into a 30, and so on. There are also "cheater electrical plugs" which allow you to use two adjacent 15 amp circuits to get 30 amps (especially useful in Mexico).

Housewares

It simplifies the packing procedure if the RV has its own bedding and kitchenware.

Often in the Sunbelt, and certainly en route, you need blankets or sleeping bags. A **heater,** where you use the park's electricity, will conserve propane (used by the furnace). Propane-powered catalytic heaters can operate when electricity is unavailable.

Corelle **dishes** are ideal for RV travel–attractive but inexpensive, microwavable, virtually unbreakable, and grease-resistant (removes easily). Corelle does away with the need for coffee filters or paper towels between dishes and bubble wrap around mugs and glasses when traveling. Settings for four are usually adequate, with paper plates on hand for larger gatherings, but extra cutlery is often needed. Take along the appropriate dish for your favourite potluck recipe. With no dishwasher, you need a small plastic dish rack.

Lightweight stacking aluminum pots and pans with interchangeable lids are recommended, as well as a frying pan, toaster, and kettle. Many cooking items are personal. I need my muffin tins and stir fry pan. Many RVers use slow cookers and George Foreman Grills.

Cupboards and the refrigerator should be packed according to frequency of use, with heavy items on lower shelves, and tall items at the back. Extra plastic shelving and bins help with organization in large cupboards. Scoot Guard (rubber-like shelf liner) and/or towels (stuffed in) will prevent items from sliding or falling in transit, although with tightly packed storage shifting is not an issue.

Don't forget towels—hand, bath, and dish. Also, wash and dish cloths, and paper products. Towels in place of a bath mat are more easily stored and laundered. A removable spring bar in the **shower** provides hanging space for wet (and bulky, if closet space is limited) clothing. Waste receptacles for the kitchen and bathroom are required, as well as a compact vacuum cleaner, broom, and dust pan.

For **outdoor living** you should have a grill, propane source, and butane lighter; a door mat and patio rug; folding chairs, recliner(s), and a collapsible table (most snowbird parks do not have them). Sunbelt resorts also do not have fire pits, but portable ones can be purchased. And now available a Wallup Wall-in-a-Bag (a portable privacy screen) and a Spa 2 Go (a portable hot tub!).

Electronic Devices

A **TV** cable is necessary for all but local programming, and a further adaptor is needed for non-digital televisions. Many snowbirds have a satellite dish (free-standing or rooftop) for extended coverage, Shaw Direct considered the best system for accessing Canadian channels.

CB radios are useful for learning about weather, radar traps, road conditions and hazards; when you are traveling in a convoy; or in case of a highway emergency. They can also be a source of entertainment. RVers usually use channel 13 and truckers 17, 19, and 21. Channel 9 is for emergencies. The number you monitor should be posted on the back of your rig.

Walkie talkies are handy for short range communications–while parking, in the campground, shopping mall, etc. **Global positioning systems** are popular for staying on the right road (and with handheld ones, for geo-caching).

A **cellphone** is a necessity, if only for emergency use. A **computer** is now considered standard equipment with long-term RVers–for e-mail, business transactions, games, and information. (See previous chapter.)

A **weather radio** with back-up batteries, turned on 24/7, is the quintessential meteorological warning device. For alerts on weather in the United States, the country with the world's greatest weather extremes, the radio should be purchased there.

Miscellaneous

Wooden or plastic **leveling blocks** are necessary for trailers, for motorhomes without a more sophisticated system, and for all rigs on soft surfaces. A **bubble level** simplifies the leveling procedure. Fifth wheels and trailers also need stabilizing **jacks** and wheel **chocks** (the latter also advisable for motorhomes when parked on a slope). Jack pads will also prevent sinking in soft terrain.

Vent covers allow you to travel with roof vents open for air circulation.

Folding **bikes** are available, but with the regular kind you will need a rack and ideally a cover (tarps are cheaper and often easier to use, with bungee cords, than custom-made ones). A golf ball on the end of a kickstand will prevent it from sinking into sand.

Most fifth wheels and some trailers and motorhomes require a **portable step** at the entry door.

Eventually you will need **washing equipment**–a ladder, a hose with a pistol grip, a long-handled brush and squeegee, bucket, and cloths for drying. There are dozens of products to clean and protect your rig, roof, and awning, including several which claim to remove the infamous black streaks. **California dusters** are good for a quick once-over to remove dry sand in windy locales.

Tire covers will help protect your expensive tires from the sun. **Awning tie-down kits** will offer some protection from wind gusts, but don't rely on them when you leave for any length of time. A **hitch-lock** will prevent someone from driving off with your fifth wheel.

Bungee cords have myriad uses–from wrapping around sleeping bags and bicycle tarps to holding screen doors open and cupboard doors closed. Zip-Lock bags and hair dryers are also multi-purpose staples.

It has been said: "You only need two tools—**WD-40** and **duct tape.** If it doesn't move and should, use the WD-40. If it moves and shouldn't, use the tape." A recent e-mail listed "43 Uses for WD-40" (all serious) and it is apparently also a legal alternative to pepper spray.

Personal Items

Assemble your passport (should be valid for six months after your departure date); provincial and out-of-country insurance cards; up-to-date cards for AAA, discount and RV clubs, etc.; receipts for expensive jewelry, cameras, and such; and your maps and guidebooks. Make two **photocopies** of valuable cards and papers–one set for a contact person back home and one to go in the rig. You can get a valise-style fireproof **safe** (at Walmart) for about $20.

In addition to insurance cards, those with health problems should carry copies of their medical history, a list of medications with times and doses, and, if relevant, a copy of their most recent electrocardio-gram. Time is often vital in medical emergencies.

As exhorted by experienced travelers (with the exception of cruisers)–do not take too many **clothes**. RV snowbirds are a casual bunch. One Sunday-go-to-meeting outfit is enough, even if you are in one location all winter. Choose lightweight items which are comfortable, easily washable, and do not need ironing. Include a brimmed hat, sturdy walking shoes, waterproof footwear and jacket, a sweater, and of course a bathing suit (you won't be intimidated by buff bods in a snowbird pool).

Pack favourite **food** items you think may be unavailable on your trip, as well as some basic groceries, but be aware certain fruits and some meats will be confiscated at the border. (See next chapter.) Consider that cereal and soups for some reason are considerably more expensive in the United States.

If possible carry enough prescription **medication** (in the original containers) for the duration of your trip, an extra pair of glasses, and prescriptions for both. Also, sunglasses and sunscreen.

Pets need an up-to-date immunization certificate (plus a recent health certificate for Mexico), bedding, grooming supplies, medication (possibly including heartworm and flea control), a leash, toys, and animal toiletries (a supply of doggie bags or a litter box and litter). And of course food.

Don't forget your camera, binoculars, an umbrella, a small sewing kit, first aid supplies, a flashlight, candles, matches, cards, games, CD's, videos, and your address book. What you overlook is most likely available in your friendly 24-hour Walmart SuperCenter.

Take care to distribute weight evenly when packing the RV.

The Great Toilet Paper Debate

Not since the prolonged dispute among 15,000 Ann Landers readers on the correct way to hang the toilet roll, has there been such a controversy. The dilemma for RVers is whether to spend $4.44 for four rolls of Thetford 2 ply at Camping World or $5.99 for 12 rolls of Purex at Walmart. At issue is whether cheaper brands will clog the RV's plumbing system.

Studies by concerned campers have been documented in RV trade publications, such as the one by Graham Gore outlined in an issue of the *RV Times* with six brands of tissue in paper beer mugs of water. A simple test, recommended by the "Super Flusher" sales person/holding tank expert at Indian Waters RV Resort, is to put two sheets of toilet tissue into a large glass half full of water for ten minutes and then shake. If the paper breaks down well it is okay for RV usage. Another criterion is whether or not you can stick your finger through a piece of wet tissue.

Most brands pass the above tests but, interestingly, it is claimed that two ply is actually preferable to one ply, because it has "less bonding material". The overall consensus seems to be that if using a minimal amount of water when flushing, as when boondocking long-term, a biodegradable product is worth the extra cost, but in most cases, more important than the type of toilet paper is using chemicals in the black water tank to break down solids and dumping only when the tank is at least ¾ full.

Most RVers use whatever is on sale with no problems.

When the rig is fully packed, add ¼ tank of freshwater (more if you will be dry camping), a gallon or two in each of your waste tanks, a tank of gas and propane, and then check your axle weights at a truck scale. Redistribute (or unload) items if necessary. Also check your tire pressure.

Turn on the RV fridge the day before you leave.

Now—it's show time!

Gentlemen, Start Your Engines

And you're off! Only U.S. Customs, a thousand some odd miles of blacktop, and a possibly a few weather glitches between you and snowbird country.

Crossing Mile Zero

At border crossings use the lanes designated for automobiles rather than trucks, but expect a tight squeeze at the booth, which in most cases was set up before wide-body RV's. It's a good idea to fold in your mirrors. Watch for signs to indicate if one lane is higher. Be prepared for a wait–especially on holiday weekends.

RVers are subject to more questions and searches than drivers of automobiles. Be polite, patient, and straightforward (no wise-cracks or sarcasm). Dave Hunter, author of *Along I-75*, recommends you remove your sunglasses and turn off your engine, but I question the latter suggestion. Going south you will most likely be asked to pull over further along for a review of your grocery items, and going north probably waved through after a few standard queries.

Be prepared to allow an inspection of the rig–without your presence, and perhaps with dogs. The level of scrutiny will vary from trip to trip and official to official. After some bad press a few years back, those at the Washington border stations were given a briefing on public relations.

All land travelers to and from the U.S. must now have a passport, or at least an enhanced driver's license or Nexus pass. (Although Nexus works in some airports, a passport is usually required for air travel.) Also be prepared to give customs officials proof of a permanent address, such as a tax or utility bill, as assurance that you intend to return to Canada. If you are a full-timer do not volunteer the information. When asked, give your immediate destination. "South" is not good enough. It is written pets require up-to-date immunization records, although Simba's were never checked.

Valuables, such as a computer, expensive camera, jewelry, etc., without an accompanying receipt, should be registered at the border on a form Y38.

Keep sales slips for all cross-border purchases, bearing in mind that your under-duty limit after seven days (in 2011) is $750 Canadian per person. Replacement parts for the RV, car, or truck must be included in the total, although emergency repairs may be waived. Restrictions of 1.14 litres of liquor, 1.5 litres of wine, or two dozen beer, are the same south- and north-bound. Check out www.cbp.gov or phone U.S. customs for up-to-date policies on homemade wine. Be honest with declarations—credit card records can reveal unclaimed items.

There is something about going through customs that can bring fear into the heart of the most law-abiding citizen. On the other hand, I know of a couple who returned from Mexico with their freshwater tank full of Vodka. Not recommended.

You Can't Take it With You

With the Avian Flu scare and cases of Mad Cow Disease in 2004, there ensued a more thorough inspection of recreational vehicles entering the United States. I was devastated that summer when the American border patrol officer wanted to seize my homemade cabbage rolls, lasagna, and chili, as well as Simba's processed dry diabetic dog food in an unopened package.

Living near the border, we returned home dejectedly, stuffed our rejected foodstuffs into the freezer, tracked down made in the U.S. dog food, and opened a bottle of wine—glad we didn't live in Kamloops. The next day we would try again.

Things have changed greatly since then, and now really all one has to worry about is citrus and tropical fruits, lamb, and pet foods containing lamb, sheep, or goat. If in doubt check with U.S Customs and Border Protection at 703 526-4200 or http://cbp.gov.

Highways and Byways

Good **maps** (ideally with exit numbers as in *Rand McNally*) are essential for unfamiliar routes and should be studied by the navigator and driver together each day before setting out. Be prepared for a discrepancy between maps and street signs on thoroughfares in major cities—as in Fort Myers, Florida, where Highway 4 is also Tamiami Trail or Cleveland Avenue—depending on your location. Many RVers now have GPS's, although apparently they are not always accurate and sometimes send you down one-way streets.

As previously noted, *The Next Exit* is invaluable for locating supermarkets, restaurants, and gas outlets near interstate exits, indicating rest areas, RV-sized fuel outlets and adjacent eateries, Walmarts, and Cracker Barrel restaurants in bold print. I think they should also highlight Camping Worlds, but I guess the guide caters to truckers as well, who would not be interested in sewer hoses and biodegradable toilet paper. *Exit Now: Interstate Exit Directory* is an alternative source of information. *The Mountain Directory* (there are east and west versions) is recommended for anticipating (or avoiding) mountain grades and passes.

Novelist/TV host/highwayman Charles Kurault has been quoted as saying, "Thanks to the **Interstate Highway System** it is now possible to travel from coast to coast without seeing anything", but to get from Point A to Point B, the network works well. Highway signage on the interstates is excellent and exits are well-marked, many states identifying businesses which can accommodate big rigs with yellow circles with "RV" in the center. Roadside emergency **call boxes** can usually be found every mile or so near large cities, and at regular intervals all along I-75 and I-95 in Florida, but it has been reported the boxes are sometimes monitored by criminals.

Rest areas are available about every forty miles along the interstates —the distances varying from state to state, and according to the number of cities and traffic volume along the route. The rest stops have pleasant settings, good parking (although sometimes tight around noon in the truck/RV section), washrooms, picnic tables, pet areas, usually telephones, and sometimes a dump station.

Although many states allow overnighting, it is not recommended as rest areas are notorious for crimes after dark, with locations next to freeways ideal for a quick getaway. After several rest stop murders, most in Florida have 24-hour security. Unfortunately some rest areas are being closed for budgetary reasons.

East-west interstates are designated with even numbers (the main ones ending in "0") and increase in number from the south. North-south interstates are named with odd numbers, with the main ones ending with "5", and increase in number from the west. Three-digit numbers are used for bypasses or ring-roads–I-405 the Seattle bypass and I-205 the Portland bypass for I-5. Turnpikes and bypass roads usually use consecutive numbers, rather than mileage indicators, for exits.

Although the American highway system is impressive, the multi-lane and often multi-level freeways near big cities can be intimidating, particularly to drivers of large RV's. The velocity of the traffic seems directly proportional to the number of levels, lanes, and trucks. (When possible drive in a center lane to avoid merging traffic.) Particularly daunting is the labyrinth of LA freeways, which can have as many as 22 lanes, and is best avoided.

Freeway intersection with call box

Many RVers shun the often stressful interstates in favour of slower, less busy, truckless routes, where signs won't be blocked by an 18-wheeler. When traveling secondary highways it is important to know the height (including the air conditioner) and weight of your RV for tunnels, underpasses, and bridges. It is recommended the dimensions be posted on the sun visor. On single-lane roads pull over whenever possible to let vehicles pass.

In many smaller cities there are frontage roads parallel to the freeway and often in larger ones there are signs promoting U-turns at major intersections (for the runabout vehicle, not the rig). In areas prone to flash flooding watch for dips (for runoff) at intersections and parking lot exits, which may scrape your hitch on the dinghy or overhang of your motorhome. Often outside lanes are less dippy.

Visitor centers, often located on the interstates near statelines, are valuable sources for discount coupon booklets, information pamphlets, and personalized information from the person on duty.

Signs against picking up hitchhikers usually indicate the proximity of prisons. Checkstops for illegal Mexican aliens are common in southern California and Arizona. Southern Florida has signs indicating crocodile and panther crossings.

Pit Stops

RV fuel stops must be chosen with care, for easy in and out. Scrutinize the location of the pumps, the height of overhangs, and exits for latitude, angles and dips before committing yourself. A challenge while traveling at 60 miles an hour.

Of the regular gas stations in the western states, Arco consistently offers the best price, but many of their outlets are not built for big rigs and most do not accept credit cards. U.S fuel prices are often higher for non-cash purchases.

In recent years there have been problems for Canadians paying for fuel with plastic, as many pumps now ask for a (five-digit) zip code. It is reported to work if you use the numbers of your Canadian postal code (delete the letters) and add two zeros to the end (V3S0K1 becomes 30100). Other alternatives are to pay by debit card (if accepted), send your co-pilot inside with the credit card, or pre-pay a pre-determined amount. Never leave your card unattended.

TA (TravelCenters of America), Flying J, Love's, and Pilot **Travel Centers**, with lots of room at the pumps, as well as good prices, restaurants, stores, clean washrooms, and often dump stations, telephones, and free wi-fi, are always the best choices for RVers along the interstates. Occasionally another gas brand is advertised on signage, rather than "Flying J", "Pilot", etc.–making them difficult to spot.

Many of Flying J's 250+ locations have one-stop "islands", with gas, diesel, and propane, especially for RV's. Surprisingly, in 2008 because of the drop in the price of oil and freezing of credit, the company filed for Chapter 11 Bankruptcy Protection. In 2009 Pilot acquired all their locations but agreed to keep the original name.

The Next Exit or *Exit Now* guidebooks are invaluable for planning fuel stops. If you don't know the whereabouts of the next super-size gas station, it is a good idea not to let the tank get lower than half. Use the entrance for "RV's and Autos", rather than the one for "Trucks", unless you want diesel.

Not all service stations have **propane**, but most large RV parks sell it on site and many offer delivery. The convenience is worth the extra cost.

Air usually costs money–when you are able to find a workable pump (the hoses are often vandalized). Truck stops are your best bet. Consider carrying a small air compressor for emergencies.

Service station **washrooms** in the southern United States are infamous for their unsanitary conditions, and some establishments offer no customer facilities at all. (To avoid possible criminal acts therein?) On the other hand, many states require that public restrooms provide disposable paper toilet seat covers, although the dispensers are often empty.

For optimum mileage, drive in the right-hand lane at 55 miles per hour, ignoring those zooming past at 70 or 80. Truck drivers with tight schedules can be particularly aggressive, but on the other hand truckers will usually flash their lights when it is safe for you to return to the right lane after passing or to say thanks when you have pulled over for them. Monitoring your tire pressure and using your roof air and generator, rather than dash air, will also conserve fuel.

Beware of Active Weather

The United States is recognized as "the most severe weather prone country on earth". In Canada TV weather segments have names such as "Skyscan" or "Sky Tracker": in many U.S. locations they are "Storm Watch" or "Storm Tracker" and weather reporters are the "Storm Team". Stay aware of the meteorological conditions along your route and be prepared to leave a day or two early or to sit out the storms.

GETTING THERE IS HALF
THE FUN–OR NOT

It's a great feeling motoring down the highway towards new adventures and favourite destinations, surrounded by ever-changing vistas. But being aware of what lies ahead can avert possible calamity.

Our Rookie Trip

When winter finally relaxed its snowy grip on the West Coast in early 1996 we embarked on our initial RV trek south–to Texas. Our Triptik and dozens of maps and guidebooks attested to our grand intentions. San Antonio to be exact–the Riverwalk and Alamo.

Once our plastic pineapple, artificial grapes, and overripe banana had passed inspection at the Peace Arch border crossing, we filled up on low-priced U.S. gas ($1.13 a gallon!), and stocked up on service station milk, cheese, and eggs in Blaine (bargain-priced to attract British Columbians crossing the border to buy cheap fuel).

After a late start, our usual (but not recommended) style, we called it a day 176 miles down I-5, at the Peppertree Motel and RV Park in Centralia, Washington, noted for its factory outlet stores. At nine, Paul set the bathtub tap to a slow drip so the water lines wouldn't freeze, we crawled into bed, and were soon lulled off to sleep by the steady roar of trucks.

At dawn I was surprised to see the freeway was almost deserted. Strange that truckers took Sunday off, I thought. We were on the road before eight, the sun was shining, and we felt great. A few miles into our journey our spirits sagged, however, when we spied a sanding truck in one of the northbound lanes and then a semi-trailer in the ditch on our side. Apparently driving conditions were less than perfect.

In fact the highway was extremely slippery. The traffic ahead crawled along the normally high-speed route. I was terrified. Paul's hands tightened on the steering wheel. Simba, our fearless lhasa-poo, watched the road anxiously from her post on my lap.

Luckily when an easy exit to a truckstop presented itself we were able to glide off the road to safety. After watching the back wheels of an eighteen-wheeler pulling in ahead slide to within inches of the ditch, we made hot chocolate and set up the Scrabble, glad to be in the Bounder rather than a Toyota. Before long the trucks began pulling out and we followed.

An hour or so later, however, on the Portland bypass, we again noted a scarcity of vehicles. When it finally occurred to us to turn on the radio, we heard warnings to stay off city streets because of an overnight ice storm. Great! The bypass road had been sanded, however, and with almost no traffic to contend with, we continued slowly into central Oregon, trying to ignore the dozens of abandoned vehicles resting in the ditches along the route. We had learned the importance of staying informed of weather conditions.

The third day was easy going, although I observed that many fields were under water and river levels were high. In Medford a bike path disappeared into a watery channel. Checking the road conditions for the Siskiyou Pass on TV after overnighting in Talent, we were informed that weather to the south was good, but that communities to the north, including Portland, were bracing for serious flooding. Some sections of I-5 had been closed. We were thankful we had not set out a day later.

Across the mountains we were greeted by an agricultural inspection station asking about citrus fruits and by the warm Californian sun. The butter in the cupboard was spreadable. We started to feel like snowbirds.

Just south of Sacramento the next day the sun disappeared however, and we found ourselves in a grey tunnel flanked by an endless stream of trucks. The Triptik confirmed that Interstate 99 is a "busy truck route" and that "the San Joaquin Valley between Sacramento and Bakersfield regularly experiences heavy fog during the winter months". (I later learned that schools in the area routinely dictate fog delays in winter.) The I-99 road surface, too, left much to be desired, and Paul seemed to be forever changing lanes for merging traffic in the numerous population centers we passed through. I made a mental note to read the highway travel guides *before* heading out.

Across the Tehachapi Pass the following day, we were embraced by the blue skies of the Mojave Desert but I was disheartened by the great expanse of barren, dun-coloured terrain, with scrubby bushes here and there, but no cactuses. Only the roadside litter added colour and interest to the scene. I contemplated the connection between "desert" and "deserted", and wondered why people would choose to winter in such a place.

I also mused that the substantial rumble strips on the side of the road had probably saved the lives of many a dozing driver hypnotized by the monotony of the landscape, and wondered how many summer travelers had become dehydrated and perished along this desolate stretch of highway after their transmission or air conditioner died. I suggested we call it a day and stop in Barstow for the night.

On our way to Needles the next morning we met up with the southern California winds for the first time. The Bounder veered to the right, Paul tightened his grip on the steering wheel, and I prayed. Simba watched the road anxiously. The Triptik warned that there was no gas for 120 miles but indicated there was a rest stop about thirty miles down the road. When we finally reached the sought-after green sign, our relief was quashed, however, by a sticker proclaiming "Rest Area Closed" and barriers across the entrance road. I could understand closing the washrooms if there was a water problem, but the whole rest area? We pulled onto the shoulder and psyched ourselves up for the last blustery leg of our trip.

Needles is a nondescript haphazardly planned town on Route 66, whose main attribute seems to be its proximity to Laughlin, Nevada (Little Las Vegas), but we were delighted to get to the CRA Northshore Resort where we could relax for a couple of days before heading on to Lake Havasu, an hour down the road.

After encountering snow, freezing rain, floods (almost), dense fog, and killer winds, we decided we would do the Riverwalk another time. This year Arizona would do just fine.

Blowing in the Wind

It attacked Two Springs RV Resort in North Palm Springs in the dead of night, its force almost toppling the Bounder. I was terrified. Simba the lion-hearted whimpered up front in her Pet Voyager. Even Paul was wakened, and brought our shivering baby into bed with us.

Simba the Lion-hearted

I turned on the radio to get emergency procedures, but found only the mellow music of the 40's and 50's so popular in Palm Springs. The disc jockey had probably vacated his post to head for shelter. I peered out the window to observe the evacuation of fellow RVers, but saw nothing but ominous blackness and genuflecting palms.

After a few snatches of stressful sleep, at six we turned on the television for the early morning newscast. Following a rundown on the local murders and earthquakes, the announcer commented nonchalantly that "windy conditions" would continue for another day.

"Windy conditions"? They were at least category 3 hurricane force!

It was now clear why no one had taken the prime parking spot with the wonderful mountain vista on our south side. They were all familiar with the windy conditions in the dry camping area of the desert park. We were left as an unsuspecting buffer to enjoy our view of Mt. San Jacinto.

Because of the windy conditions we altered our plans to head to Arizona that day, and pointed the Saturn south through the blowing sand on Gene Autry Drive towards Palm Springs. After an interesting day cruising up and down impressive palm-lined streets with names such as Bob Hope Drive, Dinah Shore Drive, and Frank Sinatra Boulevard, on the homeward trip I marveled at the thousands of windmills on our left rotating at breakneck speed. I learned later that NASA has declared the San Gorgino Pass, northwest of Palm Springs, one of the most consistently windy places on earth.

On our travels over the next month we frequently noted freeway signs warning, "Blowing Dust Area" or "High Wind Area". One suggested that when lights were flashing drivers should pull off the road and delay their travel plans. But there was nowhere to do so, and the next rest area, thirty miles down the road, was closed!

At a later stay at Lake Perris, the Los Angeles television stations often spoke of Santa Ana winds, which sometimes blew trucks off the road and caused sections of I-10 and I-5 to be closed. (The Santa Anas gain strength in the morning and taper off in the afternoon.) Frequent wind advisories were issued for mountain passes. It seems they take windy conditions more seriously in "The City on Wheels" than in the desert areas to the east.

Be Prepared

Because of spotty reception, television and Internet cannot be counted on to provide continuous meteorological updates. *Rand McNally* atlases and maps provide phone numbers for checking road conditions in individual states and regular and CB radios (truckers' channel #19 is the most useful) can alert you to potential problems— when they are turned on. But the best early warning device is a battery-operated **weather radio**, which even at night or in the middle of nowhere, will sound an alarm and provide information at the first indication of serious weather conditions in the vicinity.

As powerful **winds** can deflect high-profile vehicles off course and in desert areas reduce visibility with blowing sand, RVers should delay travel plans when there are high wind warnings. On open stretches of I-10 in New Mexico there are frequent signs reading:

DUST STORMS MAY EXIST
ZERO VISIBILITY POSSIBLE

If you are caught in a severe dust storm it is recommended you pull off the road as far as possible, remove your foot from the brake, turn off your lights (so that other vehicles will not follow and crash into you), and apply the emergency brake. If you cannot pull off, turn on your low beams (light from high beams will reflect back and further impede your vision), sound your horn occasionally, follow the center line, and pray. Never stop on a traveled portion of the roadway. Follow the same procedure in a thick **fog** or blowing **snow**.

If you encounter **snowy or icy roads** en route to the Sunbelt (or sometimes in the mountains east of San Diego), pull into a parking lot, rest stop, service station, or onto a wide spot in the road as soon as possible and stay put until driving conditions are safe. Be careful to avoid questionable shoulders, which may not hold a multi-ton vehicle. Chains should be carried for mountain travel.

It is best to get off the road as well in serious **rain storms**, when visibility is poor and roads are slick. Heavy rains in desert areas can cause flashfloods from an accumulation of water unable to soak into packed sand. Roadside signs often designate areas susceptible to flooding, which can be dangerous when it is impossible to gauge the depth of the water. Take care at dips at intersections and if possible avoid roads and parking lots with potholes. When choosing a wilderness camping site, consider that dry arroyos can quickly become rivers after a cloudburst over higher land miles away. (*Survivor* fans, recall season two in Australia.)

Although more common in the summer, tornadoes and **tropical storms** can hit the midwestern and southeastern states year round. Take note of the county signs along your route, or refer to *Rand McNally* or your *Trailer Life Campground Directory*, so that you are aware if a storm advisory is relevant. Hurricane warnings will usually give you time to retreat from a threatened area, unless you are at the tip of Baja California with only one slow 1060- mile escape route.

Do not try to outrun an approaching **tornado**, however, which can change course suddenly. Disconnect the electricity, turn off the propane, abandon the rig, and seek cover—in a basement if possible, or a closet or inside room with no glass on the lowest floor. If you are caught on the highway, it is recommended you seek out a ditch or other low area, evacuate the vehicle, crouch down, and cover your head. The 1-29/35 snowbird route from Manitoba to Texas passes right through the notorious Tornado Alley.

The California Santa Anas frequently whip **wildfires** in the dry underbrush into raging infernos, mainly in the fall when humidity is low and temperatures still high. One year, camped at the top of the Grapevine north of Los Angeles, we got on the road at five a.m. before a fast-moving blaze cut off Interstate 5. Another year we changed our plans to stay at Indio, near Palm Springs, because of smoke from nearby fires.

At Desert Hot Springs, California, on the San Andreas Faultline, reports of **earthquakes** in the 3.0 to 4.0 range are common. (I consider visits there "adventure travel".) Although we had felt none of them, I studied the literature on *Earthquake Readiness* in the Desert Pools laundry and was somewhat reassured to read that, "Earthquakes don't kill people; buildings do." An oversimplification, of course—what about bridges? But unless you are in downtown Los Angeles, on an unretrofitted overpass, or at the epicenter of the quake, you should be fine rockin' 'n rollin' in your rig, where you are already equipped with the water, flashlights, radio, and food they tell you to keep on hand in earthquake country. You also have heat, power, and probably a generator. Another reason for RVing.

Crises are potential neat stories, but life is easier if you can avoid them. Most of the time weather in The Southland is close to perfect. It's the main attraction. Stay informed and enjoy!

I-5 Basics

A recent article in the *Vancouver Sun* stated: "A vital commercial artery that crosses three states and links three countries, Interstate 5 is outdated, worn out and overwhelmed with traffic along much of its 2222 kilometre (1381 mile) length". The write-up goes on to describe bottlenecks in Portland, Seattle, and Los Angeles, and problems with Oregon bridges–some of which ban vehicles over 105,000 pounds.

I-5 is also the main western corridor to the Sunbelt, serving the purpose well to get from Point A to Point B, even during the winter usually in good driving condition. It is a road traveled many times by Marsha, Paul, and Simba.

Following are some highlights of the route and suggestions for fellow-RVers–regarding traffic, rest areas, supersize gas stations, relevant shopping outlets, places to overnight (in addition to RV parks, note the Camping Worlds, Walmarts, and casinos), and alternate routes. Shopping locations focus on Camping Worlds for RV supplies, outlet malls for good deals, and Walmarts for everything (including groceries at **SuperCenters**). For the most part, sightseeing points of interest have been left for subsequent chapters on snowbird destinations and publications like *Lonely Planet, Let's Go,* and *Insight*.

Highway 395 also runs from mid-Washington almost to I-10 in California, but many sections are not suitable for big RV's.

Miles (exits) are numbered from the southern statelines.

The Point of Entry

Every ten minutes "on the ones" 1130 AM on the Vancouver airwaves gives a traffic report, including border wait times at Peace Arch ("Douglas") Crossing on Highway 99 and at Pacific Customs ("The Truck Crossing" or "Pac Highway Crossing") on 176 Street (Highway 15). In addition, there are signs giving wait times—one on Highway 99 leaving Vancouver, and one on each of Highways 15 and 99 just before their Eighth Avenue exits a mile or so before the border, so that you can plan, or change, your attack. There are also crossings south of Aldergrove and Abbotsford to the east.

Border lines during snowbird traveling periods are much shorter than during the summer, although delays during prime time on weekends and holidays can still be lengthy. At least you have a washroom onboard, unlike the Honda with four preschoolers in front of you. There are several RV parks near the border for those who do not reside in southern British Columbia.

Because **fuel** is always cheaper in the U.S., Pacific Customs is the recommended crossing for RVers, who can fill up at one of the outlets a few blocks south. The Peace Arch Crossing has no easy access to suitable service stations.

Blaine was at one time a lively border-town where Canadians would flock on weekends to drink beer and watch adult movies. For years White Rock and South Surrey residents would regularly head across the line to buy gas and cheese. Then the Canadian dollar plummeted and 9/11 increased security and slowed crossings. Many of Blaine's gas stations/convenience stores closed, as had the adult movie theatres with the arrival of VCR's. Unlike the loonie, the town hasn't bounced back.

Plan to fill in the grocery gaps of your carefully scrutinized foodstuffs at the Cost Cutter on the left a mile or so south of the Truck Crossing, or at the Walmart SuperCenter north of Seattle (exit 200).

Washington

The Canadian border is at mile 277.

Northbound, exit 275 (east) is the access to the Truck Customs and duty-free store. (Liquor is actually cheaper in U.S. grocery stores.)

There are **rest areas** at exits 269 (southbound), 267 (northbound), 238, 207, and 188 (southbound), the last two with RV dumping facilities.

Holiday Trails/AOR **Cedar's RV Park** is at exit 263 (east).

Bellingham's Bellis Fair Mall is accessed by exit 256a or b (east).

The Skagit **Casino** is to the east of exit 236.

Camping World is to the east of exit 231.

Tulalip **Casino,** with a good buffet and shopping in the adjacent mall, is west of exit 200.

The aforementioned **Walmart** SuperCenter is also west of exit 200, and there are smaller less accessible Walmarts at exits 256a (east), 227(east), and 183 (east). South of Seattle there are locations off exits 142a or b (west), 111 (east), 79 (west), and 5 (east), all but the last SuperCenters.

I-5 traffic is usually heavy between exits 198 and 189 in the city of **Everett,** particularly during rush hours. Northbound take care to avoid the left lane before exit 192, unless you want to check out the port facilities.

Southbound, exit 182 (154a, northbound–watch the signs) leads to I-405, the Seattle **bypass** road, which is 30 miles in length, compared to 28 miles following I-5 through the city center. The *Vancouver Sun* article says, "Seattle area traffic now exceeds some of the busiest stretches in Los Angeles". Interestingly, most truckers go through downtown. Drive in the middle lane when possible to avoid vehicles entering the freeway.

Take exit 164a for **I-90** east to alternate snowbird routes. (Exit 11 on the bypass. Watch carefully–the turnoff is easy to miss.)

Rest areas south of Seattle are at miles 140 (northbound), 93.5 (southbound), 91 (northbound), 55 (both), 13 (southbound), and 11 (northbound). The first and the last two have RV dump stations.

Camping World, south on the frontage road west of the freeway, is reached by exit 137. (Better to go to the Oregon outlet where there is no sales tax.)

Expect heavy traffic through **Tacoma** between exits 136 and 122.

For a side trip to the **Olympic Peninsula** take exit 104.

There is a **Pilot** travel plaza location at exit 99 (east).

Exit 49 leads to the **Mount St. Helen's** Visitor Center to the east.

The **Portland bypass**, I-205, begins at exit 7 in Washington.

Oregon

The northern stateline is the Columbia River at mile 308.5.

The **Portland bypass** road, I-205, is 37 miles in length, compared to 27 miles on I-5 through the city, but avoiding the interstate bridge over the Columbia, described by the Sun as "one of I-5's worst bottlenecks", and inner city traffic, the bypass route is less stressful. Northbound take exit 288 to get on I-205.

I-84, an alternate snowbird route east to I-15, is accessed from exit 301 from I-5 and exit 22 from the bypass. There is further information on the route in the following chapter.

Main highways to the **Oregon Coast** are at exits 299a (Portland), 260a (Salem), 233 (Corvallis), 194 (Eugene), and 119 (south of Roseburg). With its backdrop of ocean vistas, coastal Highway 101 is congested in the summer, but rarely during the off-season, when there is lots of room at the wonderful state parks, which are discounted after October 1. If you can get a waterfront site, think about staying at **Sea Perch RV Park**, 6 miles south of Yachats.

Marsha and Simba at Sea Perch RV Park

The Oregon **Camping World** can be reached by exits 286 or 283 (west) at Wilsonville just south of Portland (283 is easier–then take the northbound frontage road on the west side of the freeway).

The **TA Travel Center** at exit 278 (west) is more accessible than the **Pilot** at exit 263 (west).

Consider **Woodburn I-5 RV Park**, behind the **outlet stores** west at exit 271, where going south in the fall we were given free vegetables from their large garden, which included the best tomatoes ever.

In spite of bylaw signs, the **Walmart** SuperCenter east off exit 217 still unofficially allows overnighting at the back of its lot. Alternatively use the aforementioned Camping World. Other I-5 Walmarts in Oregon are off exits 174 (east), 127 (west), 55 (west, SuperCenter), 30 (east) and 21 (west). Remember the state has no sales tax!

I have heard large numbers of RVers (especially snowbirds) often stay overnight at the exit 281.5 **rest areas**. Although rest stop over-nighting is generally discouraged, there is safety in numbers. There are also rest stops at exits 241, 206, 178, 144(southbound), 143 (north-bound), 82, 63, 45b, and 22 (southbound). No Oregon rest areas have dumping facilities. Truck stops and private campgrounds are alternate possibilities for emptying tanks, or check out sanidumps. com.

There is a **TA Travel Center** at exit 199 (west); there are **Pilots** at exits 263(west), 148 (east), and 33 (east); plus an RV-friendly Chevron and **Love's** off exit 119 (west).

West off exit 99 is the popular **Seven Feathers Casino and RV Park,** with 191 sites (104 pull-throughs!) and a recreation center with exercise facility and indoor pool. Check out their impressive website or call 888 677-7771.

The route through the Umqua and Rogue River Valleys in southern Oregon has gorgeous scenery, as well as several substantial grades between miles 90 and 68. The attractive **Rogue Valley RV Park** is to the west of exit 58 in **Grants Pass**.

The **American RV Park,** five miles south of **Medford** west from exit 21 (few drive-through sites), is the last major campground before the Siskiyou Pass. Also off this exit (at Talent) is a Walmart (no over-nighting), and an RV-sized gas station, a good place to buy enough to get you through the mountains 150 miles to Redding, California, and to fill up after the mountains northbound.

Check the weather and road reports before heading through the Siskiyou Mountains, which straddle the state line (Oregon–800 977-6368, California–800 427-7623).

California

Highway exits in California are not always numbered, but are identified below by miles from the southern border. Mile 797 is the Oregon/California state line.

Rest areas are found at miles 786, 753, 705 (southbound), 694 (northbound), 656, 632, 608 (dump station), 583, 557, and 529 (southbound). In non-summer months some of these are closed.

There is an **agricultural inspection station** southbound about six miles across the stateline. When they check, it is for non-Californian oranges.

Watch for wonderful views of **Mount Shasta** on a clear day. Expect hilly, scenic sections between Weed and Redding.

The first RV-friendly gas station in northern California is the **TA Travel Center** at mile 673 (east) in Redding. If you can't wait and aren't too big, there are fuel outlets in **Weed**–east at mile 745. There are also a **TA Travel Center** at mile 630 (east) and a **Pilot** at mile 554 (east).

There are **Walmarts** at miles 678 (east), 667 (west, SuperCenter), 647 (west), 603 (west), and 536 (east).

Old Orchard RV Park in **Orland** west at mile 619 is a personal favourite, with all of its sites drive-through, but it pales in comparison to the new **Durango RV Resort**, on the Sacramento River in **Red Bluff,** with a great pool, clubhouse, and pet facilities, west of the mile 651 exit. **Rolling Hills Casino and RV Park** is at mile 628 (west).

Highway 99, the alternate route to points south, through Modesto and Fresno to Bakersfield, leaves I-5 in downtown **Sacramento** at mile 518. I-99 has heavier truck traffic, thicker winter fog, and more population centers with merging traffic than I-5 to the west. Once was enough for us.

Mile 522, also in downtown Sacramento, is the turnoff for **I-80** west to San Francisco or east to Reno.

South of Sacramento there are **rest stops** at miles 445 (dump station), 386, 320, 259, and 206. Along this section there is also a large **Flying J** (with lots of room for overnighting if you don't mind truck noise) at mile 485. **Joe's Travel Plaza** locations at miles 463 (east) and 441 (east) are also RV-friendly, and there are a **Love's** and a **Pilot** at mile 278 (west).

Santa Nella, at the junction with Highway 33 (mile 407), has several **truck plazas** and Andersen's Pea Soup Restaurant to the east and Rotten Robbie Truck Stop and the **Santa Nella RV Park** to the west.

The straight flat route between Santa Nella and the Bakersfield turnoff passes through the rich **San Joaquin Valley,** the state's agricultural heartland. Of the RV parks along this stretch **Sommerville's Almond Tree RV Ranch** (west at mile 325) is personally recommended.

To avoid the greater Los Angeles traffic many RV snowbirds turn east to **Bakersfield** at Highways 46 or 58 (miles 278 and 257 respectively), continuing on 58 to Barstow and then onto Highways 247 and 62 south to I-10–avoiding single-lane Highway 395, the dozens of lights in the Victorville/Apple Valley stretch along Highway 18, and the San Bernardino traffic. [Apologies to my high school English teachers for that sentence.] Many going to Yuma and points east take Interstate 40 from Barstow to Needles and then turn south onto Highway 95.

For those sticking to I-5 there is a **TA Travel Plaza** on the east and a Petro Travel Plaza on the west at miles 219a and b. The former works for northbound, but unless you are desperate, southbound you do not want to add extra weight in fuel for the climb up the Grapevine to Tejon Pass (mile 204–elevation 4144'). Better to choose the Frazier Park **Flying J** at mile 205. The descent continues for about 30 miles south of the summit, much more gradually than on the north side.

The mile 167 exit (Pico Canyon Road) has a **Camping World** and **Walmart** to the west.

I-5 continues on to the Mexican border, but the last chance to avoid the Los Angeles freeways is Hwy 210 (mile 160) east to Pasadena and then south to Pomona to join 1-10.

Then on to Palm Springs, or perhaps Arizona, Texas, or Florida!

Prairie Escape Routes

The inland getaway routes are more prone to nasty weather and slippery roads than I-5 during snowbird migration periods. Always check out highway conditions and weather forecasts before travel.

Interstate 15

Interstate 15, an extension of Alberta's Highway 4, is the main route from that province to the western Sunbelt states. It is also an alternative to I-5, by way of I-84 (or 90, 82, and then 84) for British Columbians.

Montana

The Sweetgrass border crossing at mile 397 is the U.S. entry point for I-15. The route via Carway on Alberta's Highway 2, onto Highway 89, and then to 2, 93, and 90 avoids the rugged (and possibly snowy) mountains south of Helena. I-90 meets I-15 at exit 219 (mile 121 on I-15) and the two run together for eight miles.

There are **rest areas** at miles 397, 319, 239, 178, and 109; as well as parking areas at miles 366.5 (southbound), 361 (northbound), and 288; plus chain-up areas at miles 174.5, 168, 148, and 143.5.

Pilot Flying J locations, in Montana called "Town Pump", are at miles 277 (east) and 122 (east). **Walmart** SuperCenters are found at miles 282 (east), 192 (east), and 127 (east).

Idaho

I-15 crosses into Idaho at mile 196 over the 6820' Monida Pass, which is the continental divide.

There are **rest areas** at miles 167 (dump station), 101, 25 (southbound), and 7 (Welcome Center northbound); **Flying J's** at miles 93 (east) and 47 (east); and **Walmart** SuperCenters at miles 118 (east) and 93 (east).

For British Columbians coming east on **I-84** there are **rest areas** at miles 1 (Welcome Center eastbound), 62, 133, 171, 229, and 270; **Flying J's** at miles 29 (north) and 173 (north), and a **Pilot** at 95 (north); and

Walmart SuperCenters at miles 38 (north), 50 (south), and 95 (south). Many snowbirds turn south at Twin Falls and follow Highway 93 through Jackpot, Wells, and Ely to Las Vegas.

Utah

I-84 meets I-15 at mile 379, 21 miles south of the Idaho border.

Montana and Idaho have stunning scenery, but Utah and Nevada have places deserving a closer look. As the center of the Mormon Church, **Salt Lake City** and its bedroom communities have interesting architecture and cultural attractions. Southern Utah is a hiker's and photographer's dream, with entrance to the spectacular national parks in 2011 costing $25 per vehicle for 7 days or $80 for an annual "America the Beautiful" pass.

The **Zion National Park** Visitors Center is off the mile 40 exit and the main section of the park about 30 miles east along Highway 9 from mile 16. It is advisable to set up camp within the park or nearby Springdale or Hurricane, and drive the switchbacks to points east of the restricted Zion-Mt. Carmel Tunnel in the tow(ing) vehicle. The Zion Canyon Scenic Drive is accessed only by bicycle or (free) shuttle buses which stop at entrances to hiking trails. I consider Zion as awe-inspiring as the Grand Canyon.

Bryce Canyon National Park, about 2 hours northeast of Zion and 4 hours southeast of Salt Lake City by way of Highway 89, is actually a series of vividly-coloured amphitheaters populated with hoodoos of various shapes and sizes. There are thirteen breathtaking viewpoints along the Scenic Drive, but at 6000' to 8000' feet above sea level, the upper ones can be snowed in or fogged in after mid-October. If you wish to camp in the park do not plan to come by way of Zion, because of the tunnel. Although open year-round, a trip to Bryce is not recommended for RV's in the winter months.

There are **rest areas** at miles 370 (southbound), 361 (northbound), 188 (west), 135 (east), 88, and 44.

Based in Utah, there are numerous **Flying J's** along this stretch of I-15, but only those at miles 357 (east), 343 (east), 261 (east), 250 (east), and 222 (west) are suited for big rigs. There is also a **Pilot** at 344 (west).

There are **Walmart** SuperCenters at miles 339 (east), 331 (west), 319 (east), 305 (east), 278 (east), 248 (east), 57 (west), and 10 (west), plus a **Camping World** in Draper south of Salt Lake City, east of the mile 291 exit.

Some snowbirds spend the winter in Utah's southernmost city **St. George**.

Bryce Canyon

Arizona

A rocky 29-mile stretch of I-15 passes through Arizona. Time changes at the Nevada border.

Nevada

Across the Nevada stateline (at mile 122) you are met with casinos, buffets, and other tourist facilities in **Mesquite**, the Visitors' Center on the east side of the highway having information on Las Vegas shows. Consider taking scenic Highway 169/167 from the mile 93 exit in Lake Mead National Recreation Area.

The (very expensive) **KOA** at Circus Circus (800 634-3450) is the only RV resort on the **Las Vegas** Strip. (Turn east at the mile 40 exit onto Sahara Avenue and then right onto Las Vegas Boulevard.) The **Oasis RV Resort** is east of the mile 33 exit off I-15, and Outdoor Resorts **Las Vegas Motorcoach Resort** west from same exit. There are also parks north of the city and east along the Boulder Highway 93 from the mile 42 exit.

Oasis has a shuttle to The Strip, which has trolley, bus, and monorail services, but most RVers take the tow(ing) vehicle and park at a centrally located hotel (for free or a valet tip). There is free entertainment at Bellagio, Circus Circus, Excalibur, Treasure Island, Mirage, and others, plus outlets on The Strip for half price tickets to the big-name shows. But don't look for the 99 cent breakfasts or $2.99 buffets of yesteryear.

When you have had enough Vegas, consider a side trip to **Pahrump**, a pleasant town in a mountain setting an hour to the west–which in 2005 still had 99 cent breakfasts and $3.49 dinner buffets at The Nugget. There is a Western Horizon RV park, plus several others, including the inappropriately-named **Terrible's Lakeside Casino and RV Park**.

The only **rest stop** on I-15 in Nevada is at the Welcome Center in Mesquite, although there are "parking areas" at miles 110, 96, and 88.

The single **Flying J**–at mile 46 (west) in North Las Vegas we found difficult to exit in a big rig during rush hour traffic. Perhaps the **Pilot** at mile 48 (east) is easier. We noticed lower fuel prices in the southern end of the city.

There is a **Camping World** at 13175 Las Vegas Boulevard east off exit 27 and a **Walmart** SuperCenter at mile 120 (west).

California

When you cross into the Golden State at mile 298 the weather is probably acceptable, but the scenery leaves much to be desired. You are in the middle of the Mojave Desert. It gets better.

Before the junction with I-10 there are **rest areas** at miles 270 and 217; a **Flying J** at 178 (east), **Pilots** at 178 (east) and 141 (west), and a **TA** at 178 (west); plus **Walmarts** at miles 184 (east), 147 (east), and 112 (east).

In **Barstow** you have three choices. Continue on I-15 for Hemet, San Diego, or Tijuana. Take I-40 east to Hwy 95 if you're headed for Lake Havasu, and perhaps for Yuma or other Arizona locations. As mentioned in the preceding chapter, many snowbirds heading to Palm Springs or I-10 turn east on Highway 247 to Highway 62. This third option has a few hills, but nothing like the heavily traveled 12-mile Cajon Pass into San Bernardino, and the scenery is more palatable than the I-40 stretch between Barstow and Needles. Continue east on I-10 to Arizona or turn at Highway 86 for Yuma, Mexico, and various other snowbird destinations.

Interstates 29/35

Snowbirds from Saskatchewan destined for Arizona or California should head west to I-15. The most direct route from Saskatchewan and Manitoba to Texas is I-29 to Kansas City, I-35 to San Antonio, then highway 281 to the Rio Grande Valley or 37 to the Corpus Christi Area (37 and 281 run concurrently for a stretch). Those traveling to Florida have all sorts of possibilities, including hooking up with I-75, well-documented by author Dave Hunter. Passing through the central plains area of the United States, highways 29 and 35 are mainly straight and flat, but the northern states are subject to blizzards and the central and southern ones to tornadoes.

North Dakota

Interstate 29 is an extension of Highway 75 from Winnipeg, and parallels close to the Minnesota border for its 218 miles. There are **rest areas** at miles 179, 99, and 3 (Welcome Center northbound); a **Flying J** at mile 62 (west); and **Walmart** SuperCenters at miles 138 (east), 64 (west), and 60 (west).

South Dakota

I-29 crosses into South Dakota from the north at mile 253. **Rest areas** are at miles 251 (Welcome Center southbound), 213, 161, 121, and 26. All but the Welcome Center have dump stations. There is a **Flying J** at mile 83 (east) and there are **Walmart** SuperCenters at miles 177 (east), 132 (west), and 77 (east).

Iowa

I-29 crosses into Iowa from the north at mile 152, a few miles west of Sioux City. There are **rest areas** at miles 149 (Welcome Center southbound), 139, 110, 91.5 (no services), 79, and 38, all but 149 and 91.5 with dump stations.

There is a **Pilot** north of exit 1b on I-80, which runs concurrently with I-15 for 3 miles, and a **TA** west of exit 3 on the same stretch.

There are **Walmart** SuperCenters east at mile 143 and west at exit 3 on I-80, as described above.

Missouri

I-29 enters Missouri at mile 124 and at Kansas City joins Interstate 35, which heads west into Kansas. You may wish to take I-435 to bypass most of the city. **Rest areas** are found at miles 109.5 (Welcome Center southbound), 82, and 27.

There is a **Flying J** at mile 57 east on the 435 bypass and a **Love's** at 44 (east) on I-29, as well as truck stops at miles 79 (east) and 35 (west).

There are **Walmart** SuperCenters at miles 50 (west), 44 (west), and 8 (east).

Kansas

I-35 crosses into Kansas from the north at mile 235, and runs concurrent with the Kansas Turnpike (toll), from miles 127 to 4. There are **rest areas** at miles 175 (dump station), 97.5, 65, and 26. The last three, along the Turnpike, are "service areas" with food and gas facilities. Both lanes exit left.

There is a **TA** at mile 155 (east) and a **Flying J** at mile 127 (east).

There are **Walmarts** at miles 227 (east), 210 (west), 183 (west), and 71 (east), all but the first SuperCenters.

Oklahoma

The stateline is mile 236. There are **rest areas** at miles 225 (Welcome Center southbound, rest area northbound with dump station), 173 (parking area only, southbound), 171 (parking area only, northbound), 59 (dump station), and 3.5 (Welcome Center northbound).

There are **Flying J's** at miles 137 (west) and 33 (west), and **Love's** at miles 211 (east), 137 (west), 120 (west), 106 (west), 72 (west), and 32 (west).

There are **Walmart** SuperCenters at miles 140 (east), 116 (west), 109 (east), and 72 (east).

Texas

Interstate 35 enters Texas at mile 504 and passes through Fort Worth, Austin, and San Antonio. Snowbirds should take the I-37/US281 exit (158b) in San Antonio and then the Highway 281 fork at mile 72 (where the highways split) to get to the Rio Grande Valley, or stay on I-37 to get to Corpus Christi.

I-35 has **rest areas** at miles 502 (Welcome Center southbound), 492 (southbound, picnic area), 490 (northbound, picnic area), 282 (southbound with dump station), 281 (northbound with dump station), and 179. The few rest areas are indicative of the many population centers along this stretch.

There are **Flying J's** at miles 331 (west) and 274 (east); **Pilots** at 328 (east) and 184 (west); **Love's** at miles 473 (east), 368a (east), and 306 (west); and **TA's** at miles 471 (east) and 193 (west).

Walmarts are found at miles 480 (east), 458 (west), 452 (west), 414 (east), 368a (west), 339 (east), 330 (west), 261 (west), 250 (east), 245 (west), 239 (east), 227 (west), 205 (east), 186 (east), and 175 (west) all but the first SuperCenters. There are **Camping World** outlets off the mile 193 exit (west) and the 471 exit (west).

I-37 has rest areas at miles 82 (southbound) and 78 (northbound), picnic areas at miles 112 and 19.5, and parking areas at miles 44 (southbound) and 42 (northbound). There are fuel stops for big rigs at miles 130 (east and west), 125 (east and west), 103 (east), 83 (east), 69 (west), and 56 (east and west), and 36 (west). There are Walmart SuperCenters at miles 135 (west), 14 (west), and 4a (west). **Highway 281** has numerous "picnic areas".

Most Winter Texans hunker down in the area between Mission and South Padre Island—'bout as far south as you kin git in the mainland United States. A big Texas welcome to y'all!

Eastern Flight Paths

I-75 and I-95 are the main escape routes from the eastern states and provinces, passing through some of America's largest cities on their way to southern Florida. As there are few rest areas with dumping facilities along either route check out sanidumps.com if necessary.

Subject to early and late snowfalls, the majority of campgrounds in the northern states are closed from mid-October to May. Plan accordingly and, again, check weather forecasts and road conditions before you head out.

Interstate 75

Along Interstate 75 by Dave Hunter should be purchased by (prospective) travelers of this route. What follows is a basic list of rest areas and fuel stops, Walmarts, and Camping Worlds. Mr. Hunter offers much, much more.

Michigan

I-75 begins at mile 395 with a toll bridge from Sault St. Marie, followed by another at mile 343. There is also a toll bridge at the Sarnia/Port Huron access, but the majority of Ontarians enter the United States at Detroit, where the toll tunnel from Windsor meets I-75 at mile 51, and the Ambassador Bridge (also toll) joins at mile 47. The interstate goes through the heart of **Detroit**, but those coming from the north can bypass the city by taking US 23 at mile 115 south of Flint and continuing on to Toledo, Ohio.

There are **rest areas** at miles 389 (northbound), 346 (southbound), 343 (Welcome Center northbound), 338 (Welcome Center southbound), 328 (southbound), 317 (northbound), 287 (southbound), 277 (northbound), 262 (southbound), 251 (northbound), 235 (southbound), 210 (northbound), 201 (southbound), 175 (northbound), 158 (southbound), 129 (both), 96 (northbound), 95 (southbound), and 10 (Welcome Center northbound).

There are **TA**'s at miles 144 (west) and 15 (west), **Pilots** at 18 (west) and 15 (west), and a **Flying J** at 151 (west), as well as numerous other outlets suitable for big rigs (important in the less-populated northern part of the state).

There are **Walmarts** at miles 392 (east), 282 (west), 212 (east), 131 (west), 118 (west), 77 (east), and 32 (east), the second, third, and fourth SuperCenters.

Ohio

I-75 crosses over at mile 211. The aforementioned US 23 becomes 475 just south of the stateline and joins I-75 south of **Toledo** at mile 192. The ring road for **Cincinnati** (I-275) starts at mile 16. The eastern bypass is 41 miles and the western 43. Straight through downtown is 26 miles.

A recommended route to Sunbelt Texas is: I-71 south of Cincinnati to Louisville, I-65 to Nashville, I-40 through Memphis to Little Rock, I-30 to Texarkana, south on Highway 59 to 43, and then southwest on 77 and 79.

There are I-75 **rest areas** at miles 179, 153, 114, 81, and 27.5.

There are **Pilots** at miles 210 (west), 164 (west), 135 (east), and 36 (east); a **Flying J** at 135 (west); and a **TA** at 111 (east).

There are **Walmarts** at miles 193 (east), 159 (west), 125 (east), 92 (west), 82 (east), 74 (west), 44 (east), 32 (west), 22 (west), and 21 (west), all but 193 and 22 SuperCenters.

Kentucky

I-75 makes its entrance across the Ohio River at mile 193 and skirts Lexington, the only city on this leg.

There are **rest areas** at miles 177 (Welcome Center southbound, rest area northbound with **dump station**), 168, 127, and 1.5 (Welcome Center northbound).

There are **Pilots** at miles 175 (east and west), 129 (east and west), 29 (east), and 11 (west); **TA**'s at 181 (east) and 175 (east); **Love's** at 95 (east) and 29 (west); and a **Flying J** at 171 (west).

There are **Walmarts** at miles 181 (west), 159 (east), 126 (east), 113 (west), 110 (west), 76 (east), 38 (east), and 11 (west), all SuperCenters.

The **Oak Creek Campground** one mile west of the mile 171 exit is a popular stopover for RVers.

Tennessee

The stateline is mile 161.5. I-75 and I-40 run together in Knoxville from miles 101 to 84 (exits use I-40 numbering). Tennessee is the mountainous part of the trip although for the most part I-75 follows the valleys.

There are **rest areas** at miles 161 (Welcome Center southbound), 45, and 1.5 (Welcome Center northbound).

There are **Pilots** at miles 141 (west), 117 (east), and 374 on I-40 (south); **TA's** at 374 (north) and 369 (south); and a **Flying J** at 369 (north).

There are **Walmarts** at miles 122 (west), 81 (east), 49 (east), 27 (east), 11 (east), 5 (east), and 374 (south) and 379 (north) on I-40, all SuperCenters.

Georgia

I-75 enters Georgia at mile 355. All major roads in the state, including I-75, go through **Atlanta**. To bypass most of the city take I-285 at mile 259 southbound and 238 northbound. A map is recommended.

There are **rest areas** at miles 352 (Welcome Center southbound), 319 (southbound), 308 (northbound), 179 (southbound), 118 (southbound with dump station), 108 (northbound with dump station), 85 (northbound), 47 (both), and 3 (Welcome Center northbound).

There are **Pilots** at miles 328 (east), 326 (west), 296 (east), 146 (west), 101 (east), 60 (west), and 11 (east); **TA's** at 296 (east), 201 (east), and 97 (west); **Flying J's** at 320 (east), 201 (west), and 2 (west); and a **Love's** at 201 (east).

There are **Walmarts** at miles 350 (west), 336 (east), 312 (west), 252b (west), 233 (east), 224 (west), 218 (east), 187 (west), 136 (east), 62 (west), 101 (west), and 16 (east), all but 187 SuperCenters.

Florida

The stateline is at mile 471, I-75 forging through the center of the state to Tampa, after which it follows close to the Gulf Coast before turning east at **Naples** on to Fort Lauderdale on the Atlantic coast. The stretch from Naples is a toll road, which can be avoided by taking **Highway 41** to Miami. There are no Walmarts or truck plazas along either of these west-east routes, which pass through the Everglades.

There are **rest areas** at miles 470 (Welcome Center southbound), 413, 381, 346, 307, 278, 237, 161, 131, 63, and 35 (most with 24 hour security).

There are **Pilot**s at miles 358 (east), 341 (west), 329 (west), 224 (west), 161 (west), and 139 (west); a **TA** at 329 (west); and a **Flying J** at 285 (east).

There are **Walmarts** at miles 427 (east), 384 (east), 350 (east), 314 (east), 220 (west), 207 (west), 170 (east), 161 (west), 136 (east), and 111 (west), all but 384 and 207 SuperCenters.

There is a **Camping World** west from the mile 139 exit in Fort Myers and another a few miles off the freeway southeast of Tampa (exit 260) in Seffner.

Interstate 95

I-95 begins at the New Brunswick border near the town of Houlton, Maine and passes through 15 states (plus the District of Columbia) and America's densest population centers on its way to Miami. For many sections I-95 runs concurrently with other highways, including several turnpikes with tolls and limited access. Travelers of this route should invest in *Drive I-95* by Stan and Sandra Posner.

Many of the **rest areas** along heavily traveled stretches are "service areas" adjacent to the interstate, with commercial establishments in addition to services and large vehicle parking. In some of the densely-populated northeastern states, exit signs for the interstates are designated with consecutive numbers (1 for the first exit, 2 for the second, 3 for the third etc.). When there is a choice, this book uses mileage (from the southern border) as given in *The Next Exit* guide.

Maine

I-95 in Maine begins at mile 305, working its way southwest to reach the Atlantic at **Portland,** where it runs concurrently with the Maine Turnpike (I-495) to skirt the city. I-295 is the non-toll route through the center.

There are **rest areas** at miles 302, 243, 178 (southbound), 176 (northbound), 147, 117, 97 (service area northbound), 83 (service area southbound), 59 (service area both lanes), 24 (service area both lanes), and 3 (Welcome Center northbound).

There are **fuel stops** for large rigs at miles 302 (west), 244 (west), 180 (west), 157 (west), 132 (west), 75 (east), and 2 (east), all but the one at mile 180 operated by Canada-based Irving Oil.

There are **Walmarts** at miles 302 (west), 187 (west), 157 (west), 130 (east), 112 (east), 44 (east), and 32 (east), all but 302, 187, and 44 SuperCenters.

New Hampshire

I-95 cuts the southeast corner of New Hampshire for 17 miles, with a **rest area** at mile .5 (Welcome Center northbound), a **TA** at mile 12 (west), and a **Walmart** at mile 1 (east).

Massachusetts

I-95 starts at mile 89.5 and bypasses most of **Boston**. Access to I-295, the bypass road for Providence, Rhode Island, is at mile 6.

There are **rest areas** at miles 89.5 (Welcome Center southbound), 27 (southbound), 10 (Welcome Center northbound), and 9 (southbound parking area), as well as service areas at miles 46.5 (northbound) and 38.5 (southbound).

There are no large vehicle **fuel stops** along the route, but **Walmarts** at mile 68 (east) and 19 (west).

Rhode Island

I-95 enters the state at mile 43. The bypass for **Providence,** starting in Massachusetts, rejoins the 95 at mile 29.

There are **rest areas** at miles 10 and 6 (Welcome Center northbound), a **fuel stop** for big rigs at mile 15 (west), and **Walmart**s at miles 29 (west) and 21 (west), the second a SuperCenter.

Connecticut

I-95 follows the Atlantic coastline for all of its 112 miles, running through **Bridgeport** and **New Haven**.

There are **rest areas** (all but the first two service areas) at miles 106 (Welcome Center southbound), and 74 (southbound), 66, 52, 41, 23.5, 12.5 (northbound), and 9.5 (southbound).

There is a **Pilot** at mile 40 (east) and a **TA** at mile 55 (west).

There are **Walmarts** at miles 89.5 (west), 44 (west), 39 (west), and 33.5 (west), the first a SuperCenter.

New York

The 32 mile stretch of I-95 in the state of New York has **no rest areas**, **fuel stops** for large rigs, **or Walmarts**. Skirting the northwest corner of New York City, it does have heavy traffic. There is a toll plaza at mile 19.5 for the New England Throughway.

New Jersey

I-95 crosses into New Jersey with the George Washington Bridge over the Hudson River at mile 124, and runs concurrently with the New Jersey Turnpike southbound and I-295 northbound, merging at mile 118.

On the Turnpike there are frequent **service areas, Pilots** at miles 54 (west) and 1 (west), and a **Walmart** at 67 (west). On I-295 there are **rest areas** at exits 50 and 2 (northbound). There are **Pilots** at exits 52b (east) and 2b (east), a **TA** at 18 (east) and a **Flying J** at 2c (east). There are **Walmarts** at exits 47 (west) and 28 (west).

Pennsylvania

Entering the state at mile 51, most of this leg is through greater **Philadelphia**.

There are **rest areas** at miles 49 (Welcome Center southbound) and 0 (Welcome Center northbound). There are no **fuel stops** for large rigs. There are **Walmarts** at miles 35 (west), 20 (east), and 6 (east), none SuperCenters.

Delaware

I-95 enters the state at mile 23, with a toll booth at mile 1 for the JFK Memorial Highway. There is a **service area** at mile 5 (both lanes exit left), but no **fuel stops** for large rigs or **Walmarts.**

Maryland

I-95 crosses into the state at mile 110 and passes through southeastern Baltimore, with toll plazas at mile 92 and at the north end of the McHenry Tunnel at mile 56. The 95 merges with I-495 at mile 27 to ring the eastern half of **Washington, D.C.**

There are **service areas** at miles 96 (exits left from both lanes) and 81 (exits left from both lanes), and a Welcome Center at mile 37 with RV **dumping** facilities(!).

And finally there is fuel—with **TA's** at miles 109 (west) and 57 (east), a **Flying J** at 109A and **Pilots** at 100 (east) and 93 (east).

There are **Walmarts** at miles 100 (east) and 77 (west).

Virginia

The Woodrow Wilson Memorial Bridge crosses the Potomac River (the stateline) at mile 178, I-95 and I-495 continuing concurrently to mile 170. Although I-95 goes through the middle of the capital city of **Richmond**, the trip through Virginia appears to be a Sunday drive in the park compared with the previous states.

There are **rest areas** at miles 154, 132 (southbound), 36 (northbound), and .5 (Welcome Center northbound).

There are a **Pilot** and a **Flying J** at mile 104 (east and west respectively), and **TA's** at miles 92 (west) and 89 (east).

There are **Walmarts** at miles 156 (west), 143 (west), 130 (west), 126 (west), 83 (west), 54 (east), 48 (west), and 11 (east), all but the second SuperCenters.

North Carolina

The stateline is mile 181. The 95 in the Carolinas travels further inland than in most states, and has no large cities to contend with.

There are **rest areas** at miles 181 (Welcome Center southbound), 142, 99, 48, and 5 (Welcome Center northbound).

There are **Pilots** at miles 180 (west) and 77 (east), a **Flying** J at 106 (east), and a **TA** at mile 106 (west).

There are **Walmart SuperCenters** at miles 173 (west), 121 (east), and 22 (east).

South Carolina

I-95 enters the state at mile 198. Take exit 181 east from Florence to Highway 501 (other possibilities) to get to **Myrtle Beach** for golfing and two **Camping World** locations.

There are **rest areas** at miles 196 (Welcome Center southbound), 172, 139, 99, 47, and 4.5 (Welcome Center northbound).

There are **TA's** at miles 164 (west) and 119 (east), a **Flying J** at 181 (east), and a **Pilot** at 170 (east).

There are **Walmart** SuperCenters at miles 160a (east), 119(east), and 57 (east).

Georgia

The stateline is the **Savannah** River at mile 113, I-95 passing to the west of the capital city of the same name.

There are **rest areas** at miles 111 (Welcome Center southbound), 41 (southbound), and 1 (Welcome Center northbound).

There are **Pilots** at miles 109 (east) and 29 (east), a **Love's** at 90 (west), a **TA** at 87 (west), and a **Flying J** at 29 (west).

There are **Walmart** SuperCenters at miles 104 (west) and 94 (east), plus a **Camping World** near Savannah, (east off exit 102, south on Hwy 80, and right onto Continental Ave.).

Florida

Finally you reach the Sunshine State, which after a string of hurricanes gained a few other titles, including "The Plywood State" (for boarding up windows). The stateline is mile 382.

There are **rest areas** at miles 378 (Welcome Center southbound), 331, 302, 227 (southbound), 225 (northbound), 168, 133, and 106, all with 24 hour security.

There are **Pilots** at miles 329 (east), 201 (east), and 129 (west); **Flying J's** at 305 (east) and 131 (west); **TA's** at 329 (east) and 147 (east); and a **Love's** at 273 (west).

There are **Walmarts** at miles 363 (east), 289 (west), 268 (east), 256 (east), 215 (east), 191 (west), 176 (east), 173 (west), 129 (east), 57 (west), 38 (east), and 36 (west), all but 38 SuperCenters. There is also a **Camping World** in St. Augustine east off exit 317(¼ mile on Hwy 16, and left 1 mile at Belz Outlet Drive).

Whether you're headed for Tallahassee, Chattahoochee, Okeechobee, Chokoloskee, or Disney World–have fun!

NESTING SITES AND ONE NIGHT STANDS

Summer temperatures and sunshine are the main allure of snow-bird wintering grounds, a number of southern sun spots using the catch phrase "Where the Sun Spends the Winter". Cocopah RV and Golf Resort in Yuma offers "Golf free–any day the sun doesn't shine", but gives out few free rounds.

An estimated one and a half million Canadians travel thousands of miles each year to southern Florida, Texas, Arizona, and California (also to parts of Utah, Nevada, New Mexico, the Carolinas, Georgia, Mississippi, and Alabama) to escape northern winters. More and more are journeying into Mexico. A few head Down Under–the quintessential snowbird getaway. Some settle for Canada's Riviera–southwestern British Columbia. RV parks in Mexico, New Zealand, and B.C. are discussed in subsequent chapters on those locations.

Choosing Your Winter Destination

Most Canadian snowbirds migrate to the Sunbelt states closest to home. British Columbians and Albertans flock to California and Arizona. Those from the prairie provinces and many from Ontario and Quebec head to Texas or New Mexico. Most from eastern Canada flee to Florida. You see few license plates from the Maritime provinces in Arizona, and in Florida we encountered no fellow British Columbians.

The exact destination in the state of choice is determined largely by regional **weather** differences. In the winter coastal California gets lots of rain and limited sunshine; across the mountains, south of I-40, it is much drier and sunnier. Northern Arizona gets snow; Phoenix and south is usually delightful. North and central Texas are not warm and dry enough for snowbirds; the southern tip is close to ideal. Northern Florida gets lots of liquid sunshine and can experience night-time frosts; prime wintering grounds are south of Ocala.

Price is always of great importance for retirees with limited incomes and high insurance rates. It is largely for financial considerations that RVers stay away for three months instead of six, aggressively seek out low-cost parks, spend time on free government lands, overnight in parking lots, and limit their traveling. Budget is the main reason Yuma is more popular with Canadian snowbirds than Palm Springs, and central Florida is chosen over the Keys.

Personal interests are also important in choosing a snowbird park. Paul couldn't handle more than a couple of nights without a pool table. A bridge instructor of mine followed a winter tournament circuit through southern parks. If our friend Alan takes his trailer to Florida, he should check if the Royal Coachman in Sarasota still has a train club. Travel plans of **friends** are another consideration.

For the majority of RV snowbirds **hook-ups** are a necessity. During our time at Lake Perris State Park the hook-up section was always full, while the beautiful less-expensive dry camping area was almost empty. The vanity plate on the Monaco coach next to us at Indian Waters RV Resort summed it up: YRUFFIT (*not*–Why Are You Fit!). Desert boondockers are exceptions to the "comfort first" rule.

Snowbirds with health concerns should be near **medical facilities** and perhaps choose a winter community with a defibrillator on site.

Commercial Parks

Commercial parks vary greatly–from no-frill ones with potholes, broken electrical outlets, and grimy washrooms, to those with magnificent clubhouses, lighted tennis courts, and lakes stocked with trout. "Resort" in a park name is frequently a gross misnomer. When not referring to a specific establishment, this book often uses the term interchangeably with "park".

Many **chains,** such as Encore nationwide, Wilder and Sun RV Resorts in Florida and southern Texas, Reynolds and Sunland in southern California, and Cal/Am in the Phoenix area, cater to long-term RVers, with good facilities and lots of activities. Kampgrounds of America (KOA) can usually be counted on for good locations, cleanliness, well-appointed sites, attractive landscaping, a store, and some amenities including a pool (although it may not be open). For most, **KOA**'s are too expensive for long-term stays, but an occasional splurge in transit can be helped by a 10% discount (plus reward points) with a membership, which costs $24 in 2011.

Many commercial parks charge extra for cable and electricity (more for 50 amps) and a few for showers. Some also charge for **pets**, have breed, size, and site restrictions, and a few (notably in the Phoenix area) disallow canine guests completely.

Some RV parks are primarily full-time **residential communities**, fitting in short-term guests when space allows. Many in the sun states are retirement parks with good facilities and recreation programs, but often a population older and less active than RVing snowbirds. It is best to choose a location where the majority of the residents have a lifestyle similar to yours.

Adult-oriented snowbird parks are much neater and quieter than campgrounds back home. You don't have kid clutter–balls, bikes, inflated sharks with toothy grins, or motley items draped on lines between trees. You won't be subjected to errant frisbees, squabbling siblings, raucous music, or colicky babies. The most excitement in a snowbird park is when a 35' fifth-wheel is being backed into a tight slot.

Sunbelt parks do not have the heavy-duty picnic tables and fire pits standard back home. They rarely offer playgrounds, arcades, or adjacent waterslides or McDonald's. They *do* have a year-round outdoor pool and a hot tub to which you don't have to wear your parka, plus often ballrooms, lapidaries, horseshoe pits, greens for putting and lawn bowling, and tennis, bocce, and pickleball courts. There is always a clubhouse–usually with a lively winter activity program. Really upscale ones like Cocopah have their own golf course.

Most commercial snowbird parks have perimeter fencing of some sort, Mexican brick in the southwest, which will keep out the rattlesnakes, as well as desert winds and bad guys. They also usually have **security** gates with an attendant in the daytime and speed limits as low as five miles an hour. Many are restricted to those over 55. I don't know if that's because youngsters in the low 50's eat too much at the potluck dinners, win all the shuffleboard or pool tournaments, or play their golden oldies too loud.

Megaresorts with over 1000 sites are virtually small cities with post offices, beauty/barber shops, ATM machines, fitness centres, chapels, restaurants, bars, and sometimes their own TV station –in addition to every conceivable activity. But usually little greenery. Physical beauty is not a characteristic of most Sunbelt commercial parks, which in Arizona and Southern California are mainly beige and grey, with landscaping usually limited to the entrance gates and clubhouse area.

With hundreds of rigs packed in tightly row upon row, many snowbird parks resemble RV dealerships. Author Jack Williams has referred to them as "parking lots with sewer outlets" and novelist Sue Grafton has used the description "lined up like piano keys", but what they lack in cosmetics and private space is made up for in amenities. A large number of parks which are unappealing visually get top ratings from *Woodall's* and *Trailer Life*, based on the clubhouse, swimming pool, ballroom, silversmith shop, tennis, bocce, and pickleball courts.

There *are* attractive parks with spacious sites and oleander privacy hedges as well as lots of amenities–like the Topsail Hill RV Park on the Florida Panhandle, the aforementioned Royal Coachman Resort near Sarasota, and all the exclusive Outdoor Resorts of America. But it'll cost ya.

Any place will do for overnight, but choose carefully for a long-term stay. Study *Woodall's* and *Trailer Life* and check out the Internet, including the rvparkreviews.com website. Ideally, inspect a park personally before committing to more than one night.

Public Parks

Government-operated parks can be a refreshing change from the limited age group and often uninspiring surroundings in commercial snowbird resorts. Frequently they are visited as sidetrips on the southbound or homeward trek, or during the "week out" from membership parks. There will be no social programs, few facilities, and often no hook-ups, but you will have nature, privacy, and lower camping fees.

There will usually be restrictions on how long you can stay and, often, limits on vehicle size in parks laid out before the advent of supersize RV's. Also, the access roads to government parks may be difficult for big rigs, particularly in mountainous regions. Check guides and maps carefully before venturing too far, or use the tow vehicle to scout out the area first.

At the **national** level, there are campgrounds operated by the National Park Service, U.S. National Forest Service, Bureau of Land Management (which oversees 270 million acres in the western United States), Corps of Engineers, and National Wildlife Refuge (including free parks in the Padre Island National Seashore in Texas and in Everglades National Park in Florida). The Corps of Engineers locations, all on oceans, rivers, lakes or reservoirs, are the most developed. An annual **America the Beautiful** national park pass in 2011 costs $80. Camping is usually extra.

In addition to *Woodall's* and *Trailer Life* and the Internet, information on campgrounds in the national park system can be gained from *Free Campgrounds (East* and *West),* The *Complete Guide to America's National Parks, America's Secret Recreation Areas, Camping with the Corps of Engineers, Adventures on America's Public Lands, National Park Service Camping Guide,* and the *RVers Guide to Corps of Engineers Campgrounds.* Most are available through the Amazon.com website.

State-run campgrounds sometimes offer hook-ups and always a dump station along with their wonderful settings. Locations on the Gulf of Mexico and Pacific Ocean, impossible to get into in the summer, are especially worth considering in the off-season. *RV Camping in State Parks* is a valuable guide and visitor bureaus will have information.

County parks, such as Cameron County's popular Isla Blanca on South Padre Island, Texas are also worth checking out.

Municipal parks have proximity to shopping and other urban amenities in park-like settings.

BLM Lands

The best value for your RVing dollar–if you don't mind a few inconveniences, don't need a social director or daily shower, and have large holding tanks plus a generator and/or inverter with solar panels or wind chargers—are the undeveloped public lands operated by the Bureau of Land Management in southern California and Arizona.

On most BLM lands you can park anywhere 100 yards off the highway, with a limitless choice of drive-through view sites and as much seclusion as you choose, although some perennial BLM snow-birds expect to get their same "spot" each year. As most boondock-ers value their own space (probably one of the reasons they are where they are), it is desert etiquette not to park too close to another rig, un-less of course you are part of a group who "circle the wagons". You will be sharing the lands with coyotes, who often serenade at night.

You won't have to worry about reservations, room for the slideout, or backing in the trailer. There will be no long list of annoying camp-ground regulations, except for minimal restrictions in the Long Term Visitor Areas. Campfires are permitted.

The main negative is, with no hook-ups, you must conserve wa-ter fastidiously and break camp to dump and replenish your **water** supply at least every week or so, depending on the size of your tanks. Most serious boondockers have tote-along-tanks (aka "blue boys" be-cause of their colour), portable polyethylene tanks (5 to 32 gallons) to which you can transfer the contents of your waste tanks and then at-tach to your tow vehicle for transport to a dumping facility.

BLM campers should also have a **catalytic heater**, which uses pro-pane instead of electricity (leave the window open a crack). There will be no generator limitations, but the genset will not work if your gas tank goes below a certain level (a safeguard so you don't get stranded).

Access "roads" to BLM lands can be treacherous, and sandy sites risky. But camping is free if you move over 25 miles from your origi-nal spot at least every 14 days. Except for about $10 each time you dump and get water.

Alternatively, permits for up to seven months camping at **Long Term Visitor Areas** with limited services can be purchased for $180 (in 2011) from the BLM offices in Palm Springs, Yuma, or El Centro, or from campground hosts at the entrances to one of the eight LTVA's. Two-week permits are also available for $40. Rates increase on a reg-ular basis. BLM Arizona also offers developed campsites between $4 and $10 daily.

The areas designated Long Term Visitor Areas were chosen because of their popularity with winter visitors and proximity to roadways and facilities. All LTVA's offer some security, large garbage bins, and sometimes honey wagon service. Imperial and La Posa also have telephones, restrooms, water, and a dump station, but most LTVA campers must go to nearby service stations for these amenities. Everyone goes to town to do laundry.

For further information on BLM camping check out the ca.blm.gov or blm.gov/az websites or call the El Centro BLM office at 760 337-4400. Also consider *RV Boondocking Basics* by Russ De Maris and *The Frugal Shunpiker's Guides to RV Boondocking* by Marianne Edwards, available at frugal-rv-travel.com.

Free Parking

It has been said that "An RVer is someone driving a $300,000 motorhome, towing a $35,000 car, looking for a place to park overnight for free". It hurts to pay $35 or so for an 8-hour stopover, especially if you don't even use the electricity, and sometimes there isn't a campground when or where you need it. Plus motorhome drivers don't want to unhook for an overnight stop and most parks are lacking in drive-through sites. Some campgrounds do now offer a discount to overnighters who don't use hook-ups or amenities.

One can usually park overnight along the periphery of large parking lots of shopping centers, churches, or schools, although isolated locations should be avoided. The Walmart chain publicly welcomes RVers at their freestanding stores, but local zoning is increasingly overriding their hospitality. Cracker Barrel Restaurants, highly acclaimed by RVers, also offer overnight parking. Truck stops are noisy and smelly, but usually safe.

Before bunking down in a commercial parking lot, check with an authorized person if possible. Limit your stay to one night and do not put out the awning, barbeque, or chairs. Do not use your leveling jacks on asphalt, and if possible avoid using slideouts. For security reasons, park with your door facing other RV's.

In a bid for your gambling dollar, **casinos** welcome RVers. Some like Sunland Park near El Paso, Texas have electrical sites for nominal fees. Others, with limited parking, have a one-night limit. To the chagrin of many, Laughlin, Nevada recently legislated against free overnight camping in casino parking lots. Consider ordering *Casino Camping* by Jane Kenny.

Some states allow overnight stays in the **rest areas** along their interstate highways, but it is not advisable as a lone RV is easy prey for a crime and the freeway offers a quick getaway. Those frequented by trucks are safer. In the west, don't forget the previously-discussed free BLM Lands.

Blacktop boondocking should be carefully thought out in extremes of temperatures, when electricity is needed to operate furnaces or air conditioners. (Extensive generator use is frowned upon in public locations.) Again–a propane-operated catalytic heater will not drain the battery.

The Next Exit and *Exit Now* are helpful tools for locating potential night stops.

It is difficult to plan your first snowbird vacation. As rookies we stayed in many places where we were not happy. The second year was more enjoyable, as we booked ahead for extended stays at favourite places from the previous year and tried out parks recommended by fellow snowbirds. We also discovered the rversonline.org website which offers a list of personal favourites of the well-travelled webmasters, Tom and Stephanie Gonser.

In January, February, and early March you can expect frustrations in prime Sunbelt locations, but it gets easier as you learn the ropes and expand your repertoire of parks.

Campground memberships increase your options.

MEMBERSHIP HAS ITS PRIVILEGES

It seems everyone has a club they want you to join.

For shoppers there are the likes of Sears Club, Club Z, and Costco. For travelers there are Intrawest, RCI, and Worldmark–usually introduced through free dinners or mini-vacations, which include talks extolling the virtues of their organization and promises of great vacation savings. A small deposit and easy payments make the deal irresistible.

So is it too in the World of RVing.

Our Introduction to Membership Camping

When we bought our Bounder in 1992 at Woody's RV World in Red Deer, Alberta we were excited to receive a card giving us three days and two nights at Leisure Campground at Pine Lake, plus free steaks. Provided we listened to a sales presentation.

For $3995, plus yearly fees of $240, Holiday Trails offered free camping at several Canadian locations for three-week intervals (with two weeks' "out time" between visits). The membership could be sold or willed, and included the first year's fees in the Coast to Coast and Thousand Trails systems, which gave access to hundreds more campgrounds across the United States and Canada–for $1 a night at CTC and free at TT. As Paul and I looked forward to touring North America in our new home-on-wheels, particularly in our upcoming retirement, without much deliberation we signed up. (In retrospect, we probably could have negotiated a better deal.)

For several years we enjoyed the Holiday Trails and Coast to Coast networks, although the yearly fees at the former increased about 10% a year and nightly fees at the latter soon went up to $4, to $6, and then $8 a night. On one of our visits to Pine Lake a nice lady dropped by "to say hello" and to present the advantages of joining CTC's enhanced "President's Club" (not associated with the Camping World shopping club of the same name), and then Coast to Coast began sending information about upgrading our basic membership to "Coast Deluxe". The former option is now defunct. The latter thrives.

Snowbirds Can't Live on Coast to Coast Alone

It was only when we began heading south for the winter that we found our camping opportunities were not as extensive and useable as we had thought. Several times we arrived at or phoned a park in our Coast to Coast directory to be told that they were no longer a CTC member. We eventually learned to consult the "Resorts Update" section at the back of the bimonthly member magazine.

We were even more chagrined when we were told that there were "no sites available for Coast to Coast members"—especially when a park appeared half empty! Sometimes we were begrudgingly given one, two, or three nights—if we waited until late the first day and then checked each morning, and were satisfied with bare-bones sites with partial or no hook-ups. We discovered that at Coast to Coast parks "no" (by phone in the morning) did not always mean "no" (in person late in the day).

In time we learned the dynamics of the system, which were not spelled out clearly when we purchased. Coast to Coast itself owns no properties, but exists through relationships with parks who sell memberships and who, understandably, give priority to their members. In most such parks 85 to 90% of the spaces are reserved for "home park" members, and the remaining percentage is available for the other one and a half million or so Coast to Coast, Resort Parks International, Adventure Outdoor Resorts, and Resorts of Distinction travelers. When a resort does accept affiliate members, it is often in hopes of selling them a membership in their park.

In Sunbelt America the pressure to join other parks and clubs is prevalent mainly in the western states, and to a lesser extent in Texas. Membership campgrounds are not considered a good investment on expensive Florida land, where RV parks sell sites, lease on a long-term basis, or rent nightly at a prime rate.

Ensuring a Spot in the Sun

As we lamented our camping situation at Yuma Lakes Resort (Arizona) in 1997, where we were granted two nights as Coast to Coast members, we were introduced to **Colorado River Adventures**.

For $3995, plus a yearly fee of $300, we would be guaranteed unlimited two-week reservations (with one week out) at any of the four CRA Parks (they later added four more). The regular price was supposedly twice that amount for those with no existing Coast to Coast access, as we had through Holiday Trails.

In Desert Hot Springs (California) a week later we could purchase a membership to **Catalina Spa and RV Resort** for as little as $1295 including membership in the Adventure Outdoor Resorts system (later replaced at Catalina by Coast to Coast or RPI), with fees and "out time" similar to Colorado River.

Across I-10 at Indian Waters RV Resort near Palm Springs, where we were delighted to get three nights, we learned about **Western Horizon Resorts**, **Sunbelt USA**, and **Adventure Outdoor Resorts**, where for only $4084 (with our Holiday Trails/Coast to Coast connection), plus a yearly fee of $128 (in 1997) we could become members of all three affiliated organizations. We were told WHR, the parent company, was buying well-located campgrounds in financial difficulty and would never experience cash problems itself as all of its parks were mortgage-free. I mused that wealthy investors would want to play around with campgrounds rather than with sports franchises or the stock market. However, four years later Western Horizon Resorts had 19 parks and, in conjunction with AOR and Sunbelt, had become the membership system of choice for RV snowbirds and full-timers.

Catalina and the Colorado River Adventure and Western Horizon parks, along with hundreds of others, belonged to the Coast to Coast system, but were difficult to access in the winter as an affiliate member.

Membership Park Commonalities

As noted, to have access to the hundreds of campgrounds in the CTC, RPI, AOR, and ROD reciprocal systems (often the same parks), in most cases you require a membership in a home park, whose **cost** will range from a few hundred dollars for a resale on a single park in Nebraska, to over $10,000 for a Platinum Plus membership in the Western Horizon Resorts and K/M systems. (RPI also accepts certain Thousand Trails members, although they have no specific "home park".)

Prices depend on where and when you buy, the options chosen, and whether you have an existing campground membership. The sales pitch always follows the same pattern–they quote you an inflated price at the beginning of the session, and by the end have added extras and cut the cost dramatically. Prices of basic memberships in the multi-park systems are usually between $5000 and $7000, having increased little over the years.

"**Packages**" differ from year to year which makes it difficult to compare "deals" with fellow campers. One year at WHR there were no annual fees for life, and Holiday Trails memberships vary greatly in the number of weeks allowed in and required out of out of the system. Usually membership in one of the reciprocal systems is included in a package, as well as in a "travel club" offering access to discounted condos, hotels, and cruises. After the initial outlay and **annual dues** (often over $500), in the past camping was free, except for extra days over the contracted number. Now with some memberships there are "amenity fees", booking fees, and/or surcharges for electricity and cable.

Usually home parks and multi-park systems allow a maximum 14 to 21 days per booking, after which time you must be out for 7 to 14 days (in some cases this means out of *the system*). The number of visits at your home resort is usually unlimited and in some cases you can buy your "week out"– for around $15 a night. Stays from one to three nights generally require no "**out time**".

Although considered annoying by many, the "time out" requirement prevents "squatters" and their inevitable clutter. It also avoids a long-term association with an obnoxious neighbour. Plus you get a change of scenery. Platinum Plus memberships feature "no required time out of the system".

The majority of membership parks also offer reasonably priced **rental trailers** or cabins (hard to get in prime time) and sometimes RV **storage** facilities (also hard to get in prime time). Except in emergencies, members are not permitted to leave their rig unattended on a regular site overnight. At large parks local RV dealerships frequently display a sampling of their stock.

Cash **incentives** up to $500 or a waiver of annual dues (with a sale), motivate members to scout out new prospects, who are given two or three nights free camping (and sometimes dinners or fuel vouchers) if they listen to a presentation. (At one time Thousand Trails was giving $50 for just a referral.) It is impossible to get official information on prices without hearing the spiel and sometimes taking a tour, usually in a golf-cart.

The organizations are continually coming out with new "gold", "preferred", or "deluxe" packages to entice existing members to purchase enhanced benefits. The "**Platinum Plus**" upgrade features expanded family usage and transfers, frozen dues, and extended stays.

At one time membership parks varied greatly in their exclusivity, but with a decrease in membership due to the downturn in the economy, all have become less restrictive. Having fewer home park members, they have more spaces available for the general public, from whom they hope to gain new members. In 2011 even Thousand Trails, who previously accepted only members, their guests, and those booking a tour, has opened up some of its locations.

The slowing of membership sales has also resulted in park cutbacks, extra fees, and new promotions. Western Horizons has reacted by promoting site ownership and imposing nightly service fees, and Thousand Trails has responded by offering annual "Zone Camping", which requires no longterm commitment or large outlay of cash (see their website).

Park memberships can usually be willed or transferred (sold), with restrictions and transfer fees upwards of $400. (With Platinum Plus you can pass on your membership to *all* your children.) Resale memberships are advertised in various RV publications and on several Internet sites (notably rvparkstore.com). Check the **contract** carefully before purchasing a resale and realize that in this case memberships in the reciprocal systems (CTC, RPI, AOR, and ROD) must be bought separately.

RV resorts are limited by state or provincial law in the number of active memberships they can hold. In Arizona, for example, each site can be sold ten times. The more memberships a park (or system) has on the books, the more spaces it must offer. Parks sometimes experience financial difficulty and/or change ownership.

Membership resorts usually offer good security, amenities, activity programs, and at least water and electricity. If there are no sewers, there is usually honey wagon service and always a dump station. Catering to RVers, there are rarely full-time residents (unless they held a long-term lease when a park was purchased). A main feature of membership camping is the camaraderie which exists among members, who always speak or wave to fellow "campers" and often develop lasting friendships.

Also available are **discount camping clubs**, which require no large sums of money upfront for expensive home park purchases and no long-term commitments. Discounts usually apply to all vacant sites in the privately-owned, open-to-the-public parks, but quality and amenities vary greatly. Most of these parks belong to more than one club.

The Site Ownership Option

In 2011 although the number of recreational vehicles on the road is increasing, few new RV parks are being developed. To assure a spot in a popular location, in addition to membership purchase there is also a trend towards ownership of **deeded RV lots**. Prices vary greatly –up to $969,000 for a waterfront site in the Florida Keys!

Lot purchasers are encouraged to install a park model trailer, attractive selections typically on display near the campground office. In most cases, however, a lot owner has the option to simply use his property when he wants and rent it out at other times, or to set up a trailer of his choice, subject to park restrictions on RV size, age, and model. (Most Outdoor Resorts of America locations accept only Class A motorhomes.)

Some developments, such as the Vineyards Luxury Motor Coach Country Club near Palm Springs (where your coach must be at least 35 feet in length), include "casitas" (small houses from 500 to 1100 square feet) next to the RV pad. Still in the Palm Springs area, but more affordable and less restrictive, is Two Springs RV Resort, where in 2011 sites can be bought for around $45,000. Western Horizons has recently introduced the concept of "site specific membership", described in the next chapter.

Resale values on RV lots have been good over the years. Purchase is the way to go if there is a location you love and you can afford the down payment–plus taxes, electricity, and strata fees of several hundred dollars a month.

You can, of course, simply **rent** a spot in a park of your choosing, costs varying from $200 a month in southern Texas, to upwards of $5000 a month in the Florida Keys. Average is about $350 a month in the Rio Grande Valley, $500 in Yuma and Desert Hot Springs, $600 in Phoenix and Casa Grande, $800 in southern Florida and over $1000 in the Palm Springs area south of I-10. There are always discounts for stays over three months, and great monthly savings if you rent annually–in which case you may again be enticed to purchase a unit to leave on the property.

Decisions. Decisions. Read on for information on individual membership parks and systems.

The Main Players

RVers can purchase memberships to single parks, multi-park systems, reciprocal systems, and low-cost camping clubs–from under $50 to over $10,000. As seen in the previous chapter, in the multi-park and reciprocal systems rules and restrictions can be mind-boggling.

Individual Home Parks

Catalina Spa and RV Resort, a popular 477-site park in prime snowbird country a short distance from Palm Springs, California, is an example of a free-standing home park. In 2005 its memberships varied from $1295 for a five year term to $1995 for a lifetime charter membership which could be willed or sold, and included a basic Coast to Coast or RPI affiliation. Coast Deluxe or RPI Preferred could be added for $500. (Similar to the figures we were quoted four years earlier, and probably not too different from prices today.) Annual dues were $325, plus a new daily "service charge" of $3. Members have the option to buy the week out, space permitting, and also to purchase their own lot. Many Western Horizon members use Catalina in their required week out of the WHR system.

Catalina Spa and RV Resort

Hundreds of RV parks sell home park memberships similar to that offered by Catalina. If they belong to a reciprocal park organization, membership in that system is usually included with a purchase.

Multi-Park Systems

Holiday Trails Resorts

Canada's only membership camping club, in 2011 Holiday Trails has nine parks in its system—four in B.C. (including the popular Camperland), four in Alberta, and one in Washington (which requires an international membership). None of the HTR locations are in the Sunbelt, but membership gives access to Coast to Coast, RPI, and/or AOR.

K/M Resorts of America

Many B.C. RVers belong to K/M Resorts of America, which in 2011 has eight parks in Washington, including the well-used Beachwood Resort eight miles from the Peace Arch border crossing. In addition to the standard 14-7-14 days in/out plan, K/M also offers 5-1-5. On-site RV storage, although limited, is another plus. All affiliate options are available.

In 2006 the company purchased Two Springs RV Resort in North Palm Springs and began selling lots. Check the Internet or call 800 974-8982 for further information.

In case you were wondering, "K" stands for Kevin, and "M" for Mike.

Colorado River Adventures

Starting with four parks along the Colorado River, at Needles and Earp in California and Lake Havasu and Yuma Lakes in Arizona, CRA was the first organization to cater to the snowbird niche. They have since added parks in Mexico, Arizona, and two in southern California (the latter not on the river). Properties in the main snowbird locations are for members only in prime time, with sales presentations given at their non-waterfront locations.

Western Horizon Resorts

With numerous prime Sunbelt locations and as parent company of Sunbelt USA, Adventure Outdoor Resorts, and Fantasy Caravans, Western Horizons has been the system of choice for RV snowbirds. Its parks have good facilities and programs, although only 70 to 400 sites per property. Costs are kept down by a network of volunteers who perform jobs in exchange for a site for the winter. Several WHR locations close during the summer. Through an aggressive referral program CEO Jim Loken's system of campgrounds grew to over over 20 parks, although in recent years they have sold some of their less profitable locations (and leased back most of them).

After two previous Western Horizon "presentations", in November 2003 we decided to buy in—for the Canadian-discounted rate of $3497 US. Our annual fees were frozen at $199 for WHR and $79 for AOR/Sunbelt, and we had the option to activate CTC or ROD memberships by simply paying their yearly dues. We were pleased to later discover the beautiful WHR parks in Washington, and never regretted our decision to join.

Even for members, reservations with Western Horizons can be a challenge in high time and should be made the maximum 120 days in advance. Indian Waters and Desert Pools RV Resorts in the Palm Springs area, and Desert Shadows at Casa Grande, Arizona, are especially popular. Members are allowed two (14 to 21 day) reservations on the books at a time and then must be out of the system for a week between stays (except you can go directly to your home park), or alternatively can have five reservations with 2 weeks in between (and no home park advantage). (Got that!?!) Along with the AOR and Sunbelt USA parks, and on-again-off-again affiliation with Coast to Coast and RPI, there are lots of options for the week out.

In 2008 Western Horizons began selling "site specific memberships", starting at $13,900, plus electricity and maintenance fees. Purchasers do not own the real estate but can stay on their site up to 179 days or put it in the rental pool, and can will or sell the membership. See southwestrvsites.com for further information.

Western Horizons' Desert Pools RV Park

Thousand Trails

Founded in the 1970's, Thousand Trails, with its impressive "preserves", mainly in prime natural settings and often on water, was the first RV membership park organization. In the 1990's the company purchased the NACO and Leisure Time campground systems, and with over 80 parks in 2011 (including one at Cultus Lake, B.C.) and over 130,000 members, Thousand Trails Inc. is by far the largest membership camping organization.

Having experienced financial problems when it owned its lands outright, things improved when Equity LifeStyles, an investment/realty company with vast land assets, largely Sunbelt retirement resorts, purchased the Thousand Trails properties and leased them back. From April 2006 TTN/NACO/LTR locations have been managed by Privileged Access, owned by Joe McAdams, former CEO of the former Affinity Group, the dominant provider of goods and services in the RV industry. In 2007 the parent company also assumed management of the fourteen Outdoor World properties along the eastern U.S. coast, and in 2008 amalgamated with Equity Lifestyles properties, with McAdams as president. (He recently stepped down from that position, but is still involved with the company.)

Promoting itself as "America's Finest Family Camping", prior to its association with ELS the Thousand Trails system had few parks in snowbird locations, but no longer so. There are hundreds of types of Thousand Trails memberships available, depending on the number of days and parks included. I heard of one package offered for $17,000. Thousand Trails members have no specific home park, and no affiliation with Coast to Coast or AOR, although RPI is available to NACO, Leisure Time, and Gold members.

In 2011 the purchase of "Zone Camping" is being promoted as a low-priced option–for $499 yearly for 30 days in one zone, with the possibility to add more days for $3 a day or more zones for a $795 one-time fee for each. There are four zones in total.

I have enjoyed many mini-vacations at the beautiful La Conner Preserve in Washington with my sister and brother-in-law.

Outdoor World

Outdoor World, with fourteen parks in Pennsylvania, New Jersey, Virginia, Maine, Massachusetts, and Florida recently formed an alliance with Thousand Trails. Check out rvparkstore.com for information on resales.

Reciprocal Parks

As previously discussed, reciprocal camping systems own no properties, existing through agreements with membership parks. To join Coast to Coast, RPI, AOR, Sunbelt USA, or ROD you must have a home park (or with RPI, a certain type of Thousand Trails membership). With yearly fees of around $100 you greatly expand your choice of campgrounds (for around $10 a night plus possible surcharges)–*if* you can get a reservation. Most of the properties in AOR and RPI are also in the Coast to Coast network. Participating parks within the systems are continually changing.

Coast to Coast Resorts (CTC or CCC)

Coast to Coast Camping was the original reciprocal camping or-ganization and is still the largest. Formerly known for its annoying camping cards, in 2004 CTC switched to camping points and online reservations. In 1993 it cost $1 to stay at a Coast to Coast park: in 2011 it costs 1000 points ($10).

With a Classic Coast to Coast membership you are allowed two seven night stays per park annually, with 30 days between. You are not permitted to stay at a member resort within 125 miles of your home park, where the length of your stay is determined by your sales con-tract. Reservations can be made 30 days in advance.

A **Coast Deluxe** membership offers additional benefits, the most important of which are: unlimited 14 day stays (except in prime time when the limit is two), only seven days out between visits, no 125-mile rule between Coast Deluxe parks, and reservations available 60 days in advance. (Still not adequate in peak times.) If not included in a mem-bership sales package, Coast Deluxe costs about $1000 to add later. Yearly fees are about $50 more than for a Classic membership. Not all Coast to Coast parks are in the Coast Deluxe system.

Good Neighbour Parks are *non-membership* parks discounted through affiliation with the Coast to Coast system. They are located mainly along major travel routes in locations where there are no CTC parks. There is no 125-mile rule.

Coast to Coast is part of the company which owns Camping World, Good Sam, Camp Club USA, and many other RV-related organiza-tions. (Whose former CEO was Joe McAdams, until recently president of the Thousand Trails/ELS conglomerate!) It is now officially called Coast to Coast Resorts.

Resort Parks International (RPI)

For the most part, RPI offers the same parks, terms, and price as Coast to Coast, except deals on a cash basis. RPI Preferred is the equiv-alent of Coast Deluxe, and Enjoy America is similar to Coast's Good Neighbour system. There are also RPI Plus and RPI Preferred Gold!

RPI is affiliated with Adventure Caravans and in 2011 is the only reciprocal system available through Thousand Trails.

Adventure Outdoor Resorts (AOR)

AOR is an extended campground network established by Western
Horizon Resorts and part of its sales packages. It includes most of the
parks in the CTC and RPI systems, plus WHR and Sunbelt USA properties. Members may stay up to 21 days in non-peak time and 14 days
in peak time, when there is a limit of two stays per resort. There is also
a restriction of 3 stays at each AOR affiliate resort within 100 miles of a
member's residence, but no limit from the home resort.

The main advantage of an AOR membership over CTC and RPI
is the ability to make reservations 90 days in advance—an important
feature in prime time. Through special arrangement with Western
Horizons, Canadian-based Holiday Trails sells AOR memberships (for
$1995 in 2011). **Adventure Camping Network** (ACN) is the Good
Neighbour system of AOR—a network of *non-membership* parks with
discounted rates ("as low as $10 a night").

Sunbelt USA

The "Sunbelt" system includes all of the Western Horizon southern
resorts, as well as additional parks in Georgia, Florida, New Mexico,
California, Arizona, and Texas for $10 a night (last I heard). At one
time sold on their own, Sunbelt USA memberships became routinely
included in WHR packages.

Resorts of Distinction

ROD is owned and managed by 100 plus participating resort owners. With an annual fee of around $100, there is no nightly charge if
$25 is maintained in a member's travel account. All of the resorts are
also in the CTC, RPI, and/or AOR systems (where it will cost about
$10 a night). Because of its "no nightly fee" ROD is very popular with
long-term RVers, although there is a limit of 7 nights and two annual

visits per resort. **North American Camping Club**, a system of *non-membership* parks, offers sites for $10 with an ROD membership.

Discount Camping Clubs

Requiring no home park purchase, discount camping clubs are far more affordable than the above membership options. Of the many on the scene, the most popular are described below. All three have over 1000 participating parks, many of which belong to several camping club systems. In 2011 memberships are around $50 a year.

Passport America

PA was the original discount camping club, for years promoted at Camping World and the best value for your camping club dollar.

Camp Club USA

Camp Club is the newest member of the large family of companies which includes Good Sam Club, Camping World, Coast to Coast, and Woodall's Campground Directory. Because of its "family" connections, particularly sales at Camping World outlets, it is growing quickly.

Happy Camper Club

Happy Camper is promoted by many RV groups, such as Loners on Wheels, Escapees, Rainbow RV Club, Winnebago/Itasca (WIT) Club, Club Fleetwood, and many others.

Other Membership Groups

Other RV membership organizations include: **Family Motorcoach Association** (FMCA) for owners of Class A motor homes, which has discounts at some parks, chapters and rallies, plus an impressive member magazine; **Escapees**, which is embraced by most full-timing U.S. residents, who use their address and mail-forwarding service, as well as their low-priced parks; **Loners on Wheels,** a group of single RVers; **Rainbow RV Club** for gay and lesbian campers; **RVing Women** for women only; and **Good Sam**, which will be discussed at length in a later chapter. These groups are not membership camping clubs, but rather "social clubs" with a common bond. Only Escapees owns real estate.

The Final Analysis

If money were no object I would buy a waterfront site at Bluewater Key RV Resort 10 miles from Key West for around $800,000, as well as a western location at Outdoor Resorts' Rancho California park near Aguanga for about $150,000, and cruise around in a state-of-the-art 40' Beaver coach between the other beautiful Outdoor Resorts parks (getting an owner's 10 to 20% discount). Paul and I settled for the Western Horizon system, supplemented by Sunbelt, AOR, and Passport America for our 1996 30' Yellowstone, which was later replaced by a 2005 29' Itasca.

Outdoor Resorts Rancho California

For those who plan to be travelling for many years, campground memberships can be a good investment. Choose a home park where you want to spend the most time, or in the likes of Kansas or Arkansas, where you can get cheap access to Coast to Coast or RPI. But if you buy a new membership realize you will lose money when you sell, and consider that the average RVer uses a membership only 10 years. In 2003 we sold our Holiday Trails membership, which cost $3995 in 1992, for $1000.

Also, be aware your home park may choose to leave a reciprocal campground system, as happened at the Sicamous Sands on Shuswap Lake in B.C., when the board of directors voted to drop their Coast to Coast affiliation. Be sure the home resort is financially sound, by checking with the Better Business Bureau, State Attorney General's office, and/or park members.

Thousands of dollars can be saved by buying an **existing membership** (from the Internet or RV publications, such as *Highways* and *Family Motor Coaching* magazines and the *RV Times* in western Canada), although there will likely be extra fees in addition to the advertised price. On our resale, the purchaser had to pay $459 transfer fee (one year's dues), $125 administration fee, $500 because she had taken a "tour" in the preceding year, $500 if she wanted a CCC or RPI membership, and $1995 if she wanted AOR. Plus GST!

Read the small print carefully when purchasing a recycled membership. Contracts for multi-park systems in particular vary greatly from year to year, and one drawn up years earlier may be missing parks and features in the current organization.

Or simply plan to rent and consider a discount camping club for savings on route or for sidetrips. Analyze your RVing plans, do the math, weigh the pros and cons, and act accordingly.

THE AMERICAN WAY

Although culture shock will be minimal compared to Zimbabwe or Bangkok, life in Yuma or Sarasota differs in many ways from Chilliwack or Peterborough.

Speaking American

South of the border groceries are packed in *sacks*.

Sodas are like Coke or Dr. Pepper, not chocolate or strawberry.

Darlin', sweetie, and *honey* are used liberally–with complete strangers.

"Where y'at?" is common cellphone lingo.

In the Deep South *"y'all"* is singular, *"all y'all"* is plural, and *"all y'alls"* is plural possessive. *"Big ol'"* and *"little bitty"* are common descriptive phrases, seldom referring to age or size.

Garbage is always *trash*.

In spite of the language differences, author Douglas Coupland has written that Canadians can "pass as Americans if we don't use metric measurements or apologize when hit by a car". Or, of course, say "eh".

The Greenback Dollar

You will have no trouble finding an ATM machine in the U.S., although transactions will involve heavy service charges. The most economical way to get cash is to pay for chain-store purchases with a bank debit card and ask for "cash back". To convert Canadian money in some U.S. locations you may have to go to a foreign exchange outlet or the airport rather than to a bank, unless you are prepared to open a long-term account–which many snowbirds do if staying in one location.

Surprisingly, checks (not "cheques") are widely accepted in the U.S.–from the guy doing RV repairs out of his rig, to vendors at the Palm Springs Street Fair, to the gift shop at the Aransas Wildlife

Refuge in Texas, to the Four Paws Grooming Salon in Leesburg, Florida.

Merchandise and restaurant meals appear to cost about the same as in Canada but most grocery items are more, the actual dollar amount of course depending on the status of the loonie. Sales taxes vary from state to state and cities often have their own.

A part-time winter job would require a green card, which is considerably more difficult to get than a platinum MasterCard. Non-Americans are not even supposed to exchange work in campgrounds for site rental, although it happens.

Be watchful of the denomination of American paper currency, which is almost all the same colour.

Turkey Day and Others

American Thanksgiving, the fourth Thursday in November, is a major holiday with a four day weekend, to many more important as family time than Christmas. Public offices (including Tourist Information Centers), most retail outlets, and many restaurants are closed.

The following Friday is the biggest shopping day of the year in the U.S.–with great sales marking the commencement of Christmas shopping. It is called "Black Friday", the day from whence retailers hope to see their financial statements change from red to black.

Boxing Day, an English custom, is not recognized south of the border and it's business as usual on December 26. Martin Luther King Jr.'s birthday is celebrated the third Monday in January, and Presidents' Day on the third Monday in February.

Food for Thought

You will find the occasional Safeway–along with Albertsons, VONs, Ralphs, Bashas, Fry's, Stater Brothers, Publix, Winn Dixie, H.E.B., and Sam's Club (Walmart's warehouse store). Only at VON's, which is affiliated with Safeway, will you find familiar house brands. Some chains require a membership card, easily obtained from customer service, to get sale prices. Consider produce stands along the roadways.

In recent years **Walmart SuperCenters** have sprung up all over the country, offering a full-sized grocery section in addition to the usual departments. Many are located next to the interstate highways and open 24/7. Very handy for one-stop shopping en route, although most grocery items are not an especially good deal. Target rivals Walmart in the U.S. (Walgreens is the American Shoppers Drug Mart.)

Check the fat content on the different-coloured milk cartons before purchase, and don't bother looking for frozen vegetarian pizzas, saltless nacho chips, muesli, bulk foods in bins, or paper bags for mushrooms. You *will* find lots of cans with flip-top lids. On one shopping trip a young clerk responded to my quest for a turnip with, "Is that a kind of beer?" It *is* nice to buy Coors Light in the same store as bread and zucchinis.

The **prices** of beef, wheat crackers, cereal, and canned soups are really high in the U.S. Pack accordingly and plan to eat lots of tortillas, chicken, and locally-grown produce items—notably citrus fruits after December. Also a good deal in the West are California raisins, although they're hard to plan a meal around. (Good on porridge though).

Although most U.S. tap **water** is safe for drinking, the majority of RV snowbirds buy it in plastic gallon containers, which they later refill—for about 25 cents. Full jugs are good for holding down the corners of patio rugs, as well as free-standing satellite dishes.

At the present time **recycling** is not widespread in the United States. Aluminum pop (soda) cans can be redeemed at outlets in various supermarket parking lots for so many cents a pound, the amount varying according to your age, the day of the week, and whether you crush them, but most RVers use the receptacles at the park—when there are some. Other cans, newspapers, and cardboard, are thrown out with burnt toast and week-old spaghetti.

Golden Arches to Golden Corrals

In addition to the ubiquitous McDonald's, Pizza Huts, Denny's, and Starbucks, in the U.S. you also find Golden Corrals, Hometown

Buffets, Carl Juniors, Shoney's, Taco Bells, Whataburgers, and Jack(s) in the Box. Varying greatly from location to location. Cracker Barrels cater to snowbirds, encourage overnight RV parking, and have been named by Good Sam Club members as "the best sit-down restaurant with RVers".

Many dishes in U.S. eateries are deep-fried, heavy on salt, and/ or slathered in grease. Biscuits and gravy and corn bread are staples on southern menus, and sausage seems to be the #1 pizza topping. Popeye's is a popular chicken and biscuits chain and the Fry House concession advertises "batter-dipped deep-fried Oreo cookies". Then there is the Heart Attack Grill in Chandler, Arizona, which has servers in nurses' uniforms and an ambulance parked outside. Of course there are healthy alternatives out there.

Stars and Stripes Forever

Patriotism is strong in the United States. Expect large flags on business outlets and public buildings—notably post offices, which are usually free-standing, bureaucratic-looking structures, announced with official highway signs, often out in the middle of nowhere. Flags are also found on private residences and at park entrances, as well as on motorhomes, trucks, and cars (and on the set of *Regis and Kelly*).

Some RVers have stars and stripes folding chairs, table cloths, tire covers, outdoor carpets, satellite dishes, dishes, barbecue tools, wind socks, patio lights, and jackets.

Praises of the American soldier rival boozin' and cheatin' songs on U.S. country radio stations. "God Bless America" signs are everywhere—from truck mud flaps to the entrance of the local Pizza Hut. Can you imagine a Canadian Tire or Tim Hortons asking God to bless Canada?

The Right to Bear Arms

The accessibility of guns is a major issue in the United States. A store in New Orleans boasted: "Largest Gun Shop in the Area—Nordic Pawn and Sport". The modest library in Rockport deemed it necessary to post a "No Firearms" sign on the door, and a San Antonio tavern warned "No Firearms or Nuclear Weapons Inside". A bumper sticker spotted on a Texas freeway read: "I'd rather be judged by 12 than carried by 6." It is estimated that about 50% of American RVers carry **firearms** for protection.

Most RV parks have a fence or wall and **security** gate, and the RVing community has a low crime rate (although Gary Ridgeway, the Green River Killer, was a Leisure Time Campgrounds member for a number of years). It is nevertheless wise to keep your doors and windows locked, to have a cellphone, and to know the name and location of your campground and your site number.

Do not open your door to a knock after dark, offering instead to phone for help if there is an emergency. As one is likely to respond without thinking to someone using their name, signs such as "Bob and Peggy Live Here" are discouraged. In-park thefts of bicycles are common and we had our backup camera stolen. A park manager told of the disappearance of a shower curtain, swag lamp, money from the laundry change machines, and dozens of books from the park library (which were later discovered for sale at the weekly patio sale).

It is recommended you travel with vehicle doors locked–including the towed vehicle. In case of a minor accident, have the other party follow you to a well-lit, populated location. With a breakdown, rather than leaving your vehicle, use a white flag, HELP sign, or the beep, beep, beep distress signal on your horn along with flashing headlights. Before you give an incompetent driver the finger on a U.S. highway, consider he could be armed and dangerous.

Experienced RVers avoid **overnighting** at highway rest areas and other isolated locations. Canadians are particularly vulnerable to crime as their license plates indicate "well-to-do" tourists with no firearms on board. With a motorhome, in an attempted break-in you can turn the key and drive away (if you're not hooked up).

When **shopping or sightseeing,** don't carry large amounts of cash, particularly in a purse or back pocket. Much safer are a steel-reinforced waist/fanny pack, neck or stomach pouch, or front pocket. Do not leave valuables such as cameras or binoculars in your car.

Avoid outward displays of wealth, such as Rolex watches and expensive jewelry. Shield your card number when using an ATM. Walk away from altercations. It has been suggested tourists carry a small amount of cash in a dummy wallet in case of a hold-up.

Always use **caution and common sense**.

Only in the USA

On the lighter side, take note of the signs on your travels.

A turf farm in Oregon says, "We Just Keep Rollin' a Lawn". A bus bench in Mississippi reads, "Getting Married? Need a Minister? Call ...". Flashing neon outside a St. Petersburg office promotes, "Divorce. Walk in." A theater in Rockport, Texas features "Free Popcorn on Tuesdays, if You Bring Your Own Bowl". A Florida Outback Restaurant requests, "Do Not Sit or Stand on The Bar".

Interstate billboards advertise "Vasectomy Reversal Clinic–1-800-HOUSTON–Satisfaction Guaranteed" and "Breast Implants–$3500 (phone number)". A highway sign in Tallahassee flashed: "Welcome Spring Breakers, But Don't Break Anything".

Some gas stations advertise "Clean Washrooms", and one in Arizona goes further with "Big, Clean, Washrooms". Buc-ee's near Houston has "Fabulous Restrooms", and a Florida KOA offered "Free Bathroom Tours".

A sign on a tanker truck on I-10 warned: "This Vehicle Makes Ridiculously Wide Turns". An RV decal read: "Jesus Loves You, But I Am His Favorite".

A park model in Yuma offered: "Weeds for Sale–U-Pick".

A convenience store in Fulton, Texas had the sign:

FREE

Get a Free Ride

in a

SHERIFF'S CAR

if you

Shoplift From This Store

And a place in Vegas touted "Bail Bonds for Bad Boys".

Also check out the (free) local classified ad papers like the *White Sheet* for the Coachella Valley, which advertises items such as: "cart chariot for miniature Horse $150"; "Elizabeth Taylor-owned faux crystal chandelier, has documentation $125"; "cannon, old, on wheels, beautiful! $85"; "dolls, pair man & woman, will bring good luck $35", and a "rare electric fresh-water catfish, PACKS A WALLOP! Plays well with other fish $100". My personal favourite, from our 1999 trip, advertised the town of Gorman, California for sale. Great gift ideas for the person who has everything!

No Canada

Starved for information about the homeland I once spent more than the cost of a Mexican combination dinner for a two-day-old *Vancouver Sun* (Saturday edition). Not to mention the forty miles of gas used in the quest before we finally tracked it down at the Barnes and Noble in Rancho Mirage.

Some Sunbelt papers devote a couple of columnar inches to Canadian tidbits, notably *The Sun Visitor* in Yuma, but this is not common. And on TV usually the only indication of Canada's existence is the weather map.

As Paul signed the Master Card slip I scanned the front page of *The Sun* for juicy headlines–such as "Serial Killer Terrorizes White Rock", "Whereabouts of Prime Minister Remains a Mystery", "Street Gangs Hold Vancouver Police Force Hostage", or something of international importance, such as "Prince Charles to Wed Madonna". Alas, what I saw was: "Martin's Budget Must Woo Voters, Cut Federal Deficit", "New TV Station Planning Local Focus", "Bid to Host Olympics Torched by Tourism Industry," and "The Year of the Ox". Good old conservative Canada! But I vowed to read every expensive boring word–at least twice.

A satellite dish or the Internet is, of course, the twenty-first century solution to Canadian news deprivation.

According to an issue of *Maclean's* magazine, "most Americans think of Canada as "a giant Minnesota". It has also been referred to as "America Junior". Canadians, in our humble way, must educate our southern neighbours that our country has more than cold fronts and hockey.

More Challenges Than *Survivor*

Brochures for adult-oriented RV resorts often refer to "the sweet life" and "the good life", but as indicated in the chapters dealing with the wrath of nature and reservations for Sunbelt parks, the life of an RV snowbird is not stress-free. There are bumps along the road—and not just on I-10 in Louisiana. Challenges are often even more difficult than trying to remember which day, month, or season it is. But experts say a little stress is good. Better for you than watching oranges grow.

Location, Location, Location

Choosing your actual winter homesite can be as daunting as finding the perfect resort. Unless prevented from doing so by a Nazi-type gate attendant, drive around the park and note availability before checking in. If you are assigned a specific site, ask about a more desirable one you know is open. Paul and I once cruised around for over an hour at (the previously discussed) Catalina RV Resort before registering—Paul analyzing the lay of the land and angle of the sun, and I studying the position of trees and cactus gardens.

Size is of course the first consideration in deciding where to set up camp, sites in older parks often not long enough for a 40' rig or wide enough for slideouts. *Woodall's* and *Trailer Life* give dimensions.

For the sake of your refrigerator and sliders the site must be **level**, or made that way with levelers or blocks (with boards under *both* dual tires).

Ground cover should also be scrutinized. The larger the rig the deeper it will sink in mud and sand. (Deflating your tires will help in the latter case, providing you have a pump or air compressor.) Grass is okay if it's not rain-soaked. Gravel is good. Crushed rock is better. A cement pad is best.

Proximity to trees, green belts, and the clubhouse is desirable, although branches can be a problem for satellite dishes and fitting in big rigs. Waterfront **locations** are prime, but rare, and because of septic fields are usually without sewers. Sites near the park entrance, dump station, garbage bin, a busy roadway, or sandwiched between mobile homes are understandably not popular.

The angle of the **sun** and usual direction of the **wind** should also be considered. If possible the driver's side should face east or north for protection from the afternoon rays (the awning shades the other side).

Before hooking up check the **power** outlet, ideally with a polarity tester.

You Can't Get There From Here

Entering the drive-through lane at a fast food restaurant is a definite no-no for a big RV, as is pulling into a strip mall with questionable egress. Many gas stations are likewise unmanageable (watch the overhangs), and finding a suitable fuel outlet before you run dry can be a high stakes travel game. (It has been said: "For an RVer, happiness is empty holding tanks and a full fuel tank.") Numerous states now have RV Friendly symbols on highway signage for businesses with parking for big rigs.

It is unwise to venture onto side roads without knowing what lies ahead. Watch signs and study local maps carefully. We once turned right instead of left when leaving a campground and several miles down the dead-end dirt road had to unhook and re-hook the car to turn around—in heavy rain. Don't take the rig on the southbound lane of California coastal Highway 1 between Carmel and San Luis Obispo unless you have nerves of steel.

Houston, We Have a Problem

Inevitably the day will come when you require repairs on the road—chances are late Saturday, when service facilities are closed. The mechanically-challenged are most vulnerable.

Plumes of black smoke spewed from our Bounder in the middle of Rogers Pass, after an improperly installed oil filter. Then there were the tail lights on the first Saturn which frequently caused short circuits in the RV. And the ABS brake light in the Yellowstone, which was turned on by heavy traffic. Plus the blowout on I-5 near Stockton. To name but a few.

Be sure you have RV **emergency road insurance**. But hope you don't need it on I-10 in western Louisiana. With our first tire incident near Lake Charles on the eastbound trip to Florida, the AAA could not come to our aid until Monday, although our SOS was sent around noon Saturday. The second tire problem, on the return trip, within thirty miles of the first (those familiar with the highway will understand!), also occurred on a Saturday, but earlier, and after three and a half hours two tow trucks arrived, each with a teenage boy, who in the process of changing the tire (and chit-chatting) lost the clips to the hubcap (specially made for dual tires). At a Flying J gas stop twenty miles down the road Paul discovered that the newly-installed spare was low and that the hubcap was ready to fall off. We learned Flying J doesn't do tires or hubcaps.

It is recommended you go to a **large dealership** for repairs and get a written estimate with maximum labour time before having work done, but be forewarned there is often **no "one stop shopping"** in the RV repair business. After overnighting at the aforementioned Flying J, and in the process discovering a generator/battery problem, Paul filled the low tire and we limped down the highway to Beaumont, Texas. Sunday afternoon we spent researching tire repair possibilities, but on Monday found our first choice did only trucks. Off to the other side of town where they fixed the original flat and the spare, but could not do the clips. No place in Beaumont would address the generator/battery issue.

So we continued west to the Camping World east of San Antonio where two days after ordering clips from Oregon the hubcap was again secure. The technician recommended we go to a Ford dealership for the battery/generator problem. The first Ford location in El Paso did only trucks and the second did only cars. The third gave a diagnosis of a wiring problem, but they didn't have time to check it out further until Monday. (Yes, it was Saturday again!) So away we went to Tucson, where after several phone calls Paul tracked down a Ford dealership which took RV's. Two days and $546 later (plus a thousand and change from the insurance company) the ABS brake light was gone and the generator was usable.

I am a great advocate of **extended warranties**, the $3000 platinum policy on our 5-year old Yellowstone paying for itself the first year on a trip to Alaska. On the other hand, my sister and brother-in-law have not been happy with their extended warranty's response to a recurrent air conditioning problem, a situation made worse by their dealership going out-of business.

A warranty is one thing, but getting an appointment for your defective RV in prime time is another. We were looking at over a month at the Winnebago dealerships in both Phoenix and Yuma to fix our microwave.

As previously noted, it is difficult to get recompense for faulty parts or workmanship when you are hundreds of miles down the road, particularly from a small independent business, although Good Sam's Action Line has been successful in retrieving moneys for many disgruntled RVers. We should have pursued the fuel filter incident with the Bounder.

Put away valuables and leave your rig for the shortest possible time when having inside work done.

The Gauges Cannot be Trusted

One of the cardinal rules of RVing is "never dump the black water tank until it is at least ¾ full" as solid waste can become stuck. The sewer hose should then be flushed out by the contents of the grey water tank (plus extra water if necessary). Which would be reasonably straightforward if the tank gauges registered accurately.

Some RVers clean their holding tanks and sensors by adding half a dozen Alka Seltzer tablets, half a box of baking soda, several denture tablets, a cup of Borax, or a cup of Dawn dish detergent to five to ten gallons of water in cleaned tanks before hitting the highway. Some have "flushers" installed in the waste tanks to improve cleaning. But none of these methods provides long-lasting gauge accuracy— one tenacious piece of toilet paper or spaghetti can give a false reading. After awhile you get into a routine of dumping every "x" number of days, depending on tank size and usage. Water backing up into the shower means it's time! The "flashlight test" can be used for the toilet.

In the Yellowstone we came to ignore the waste tank readings. Always pay heed to the indicators for the fresh water, LP gas, and battery, however.

Talk is Cheap

With phone rates at an all-time low, if you use the toll free number for your calling card server, it is inexpensive to keep in touch, and cellphones and e-mail have freed up pay phones at RV resorts, where you once had to wait up to an hour on Sunday evenings. But public phones are becoming extinct, especially at new RV parks such as Gulf Waters Resort in Beaumont, which had only outlets at the individual sites, and Augie's Quail Trail in Gila Bend, Arizona, which offered only Internet service. Phone companies provide equipment based

"Can you hear me now?"

upon the amount of money collected at each location, so, little usage and they remove the phone and little potential they don't install one. Another factor is vandalism—the reason Louisiana visitor centers and rest areas offer no public phones.

Once cost-prohibitive, international **cellphone** plans are now reasonably priced—more expensive than the calling card/public phone method, but much more convenient. Desperately seeking a phone on the interstate to cancel a reservation, for which you will be charged, is a high stress challenge. With mobile phones there is of course the uncertainty of reception. You often see RVers walking aimlessly around the park with a hand to one ear, frequently asking, "Can you hear me now?" or proclaiming, "I'm losing you!"

Electronic mail has become very popular as more and more RVers travel with computers. With a **Skype** download and earphones with microphone, the computer can be transformed into a telephone— with video if you add a camera. More and more RV resorts are offering wireless Internet service.

Beware the Highs of March

When the mercury climbs into the high nineties, as it does in many Sunbelt locations towards the end of March, you plan your day around the thermometer. Walkers and bikers set forth as early as 5:30 am to beat the heat. Between 6:00 and 7:00 many rigs pull out and people do laundry, walk the dog, use the pay phone, and polish the rig. Before nine it is pleasant having your coffee under the awning.

But from nine to five outside activities are severely curtailed. Certainly there will be no one on the tennis courts, and shuffleboard and horseshoe areas are also likely to be empty. Even the golf courses are sparsely populated, as are the swimming pools, which are like bath water. I wonder if the five-star hotels have cooling systems for their pools.

In Florida humidity adds to the discomfort.

RVers withdraw into the rig or head to the air-conditioned public rooms onsite, or to a mall, movie theatre, museum, or library. They sometimes seek out a municipal park with grass and shade trees or perhaps head up the mountains where it is cooler or take a dip in the Colorado River, Gulf of Mexico, or Sea of Cortez (but not the Salton Sea). A shaded parking spot is cause for great joy.

Unless powered by a 50 amp outlet, electrical appliances such as hair dryers or microwaves should not be used in conjunction with the air conditioner. Cooking a turkey is not advised. But by 5:30 or so the sun is low in the sky or behind a mountain and the temperature drops quickly. Doors and windows are opened, air conditioners silenced, and thoughts given to a simple supper. Winter nights in the Sunbelt are usually comfortable, often cool, even when the days are scorching.

Ninety degrees is too hot for snowbirds, and the sun which attracted them in the first place often drives them away earlier than planned. The spacious well-appointed sites they drove by enviously in February, now sit empty, and the park where it was impossible to get a reservation a month ago is a ghost town.

Ants, Etc.

An ant convention in the peanut butter jar finally taught me to screw lids on tightly. Although it is said they will not enter the rig if there is nothing to attract them (like bags of garbage, crumbs on the counter, or loose lids on condiments), many RVers put chalk, powdered cleaners, or various types of commercial spray on the ground around tires, stabilizers, wires, and hoses. Some put Vaseline a couple of inches up the cords and hoses. As wet spots on the ground attract bugs, be sure your hose attachment does not drip. Avoid campsites with suspicious-looking mounds of loose earth, which could be anthills.

Other unwelcome visitors, like lice, fleas, and ticks, can come into the rig on your clothing or pet, and mice can enter through any opening. One year as full-timers we arrived back from a Hawaii vacation to find my slippers missing their fur trims, which I later found made into a nest in my tea towel drawer. It is said crumpled sheets of Bounce at possible access points, and pepper sprinkled in drawers and cupboards will discourage a mouse invasion.

The Quest for the Perfect Gift

Then there is the job of choosing the consummate gifts to take back home. Items you can't get back home and which you will not need to return.

Our first year in Arizona I spent hours choosing potted "cactus gardens", getting detailed instructions on their care, pampering and frequently repositioning them in the motorhome according to the sun, and packing them away carefully each day before we hit the road. On my first Safeway shopping trip back in Canada there they were— for half the price!

Palm Springs was particularly stressful shopping for teen-aged nephews. None of the T-shirts were cool and there wasn't a Hard Rock Cafe to fall back on. Scorpions under glass were the best we could do. Disney World and the Kennedy Space Centre are much easier for children, but close your eyes to the prices in the former.

Beware of plaster lawn ornaments made in Mexico. The colourful hombre snoozing under the saguaro cactus we bought for friends disintegrated in the heavy B.C winter rain!

Pulling Up Stakes

Remembering the pre-travel drill in its entirety is also a challenge. I venture to say there isn't a veteran RVer who has not left a park with the antenna up, entry step down, vent open, or a cupboard door not securely fastened. I heard of one driving away with his awning down. With luck the oversight is discovered before entering the freeway. Main items to remember are as follows.

- Put away outdoor accessories, chocks, and blocks and secure cargo doors.

- Put up and securely latch the awning.

- Empty the waste tanks if necessary and perhaps add fresh water (keeping traveling weight as low as possible). Secure caps and add chemicals to the holding tanks (via the toilet and sinks).

- Disconnect and put away umbilical cords (including the TV cable).

- Check tires and engine fluids.

- Make sure the cupboards and refrigerator are packed snugly enough that items do not move around or tip over, but not so tightly that heavy items can push doors open at a sharp turn.

- Turn off propane, lights, furnace, fridge, water heater, and pump.

- Put away loose items from counters and tables.

- Close windows, drawers, and doors securely.

- Lower the TV antenna (some RVers hang reminders on the crank) and roof vents (unless you have covers).

- Retract and latch the slideout(s) (after checking the path in front).

- Take up levelers, and remove stabilizers and jacks.

- Do a last check around the campsite and RV.

- Have maps and guidebooks upfront for travel.

- Hook up the tow or towing vehicle, making adjustments to the engine and gearshift if necessary, and check brake and signal lights.

- With a trailer be sure the king pin/ball and spring bars are secure and locked in the hitch, and that the mirrors are extended on the towing vehicle.

- Put up the entry step. (Ones on newer rigs retract automatically.)

A check list and/or Post-It notes are a good idea.

Dollars and Sense

Jim Loken, founder and long-time CEO of Western Horizon Resorts once said "Something happens to people when they retire. They instantly become cheap." The following suggestions can help stretch your dollars.

Before you leave home **research** destinations at the library or on the Internet. Consider buying a good budget guidebook, such as *Lonely Planet* or *Insight Guide* with its wonderful pictures, and perhaps ordering an *Entertainment Book* for any lengthy stays in cities.

Stay at membership **campgrounds** (if you belong). Buy a discount camping club membership and stay at their half-priced locations, as well as a Good Sam membership which entitles you to a 10% discount at over 1700 parks. Consider overnighting at truck stops, casinos, Camping Worlds, or Walmarts. Inquire about a AAA discount (if you belong). Stay a week, or a month, or all winter for a better rate.

Eat out at lunch instead of dinner. Use coupons, take advantage of senior discounts, early bird specials, and low-priced buffets. Ask locals at gas stations, tourist offices, and campgrounds for dining recommendations.

Seek cheaper alternatives to expensive **grocery items** (such as tortillas in lieu of bread, oranges instead of apples). Use food flyers for specials as you do at home (most snowbird parks stock them). Buy produce in season, when possible from roadside stands. Use coupons and get free membership discount cards at grocery outlets. Shop at Costco (if you are a member).

Drive at 55 miles per hour and use your roof air conditioning (and generator), rather than dashboard air, to get better mileage. Keep your tires properly inflated. Avoid idling. A wind deflector helps fuel consumption with a fifth wheel.

Use *The Next Exit* or *Exit Now* guide to plan filling up at truck stops where **fuel** is less expensive. Avoid gas stations in the middle of nowhere with no competition.

Stop at the Visitors' Center when you enter a new state to get its *Traveler Discount Guide*, other coupon discount books and newspapers, and cost-saving tips from the person on duty. Save on expensive souvenir books by collecting brochures. Use a digital camera.

Pack carefully before leaving home so you don't have to buy a new hair dryer, fishing pole, hammer, or such. When you must–**shop** at flea markets, swap meets, second hand stores, Walmart, or Target.

Bring **toiletries and medication** from Canada. Toothpaste is particularly expensive in the U.S. (I heard that you can get a few more brushings if you cut the tube in half when you think it is finished!)

Always ask about senior (in some places it's as young as 55) or AAA discounts at **entertainment venues**. Use coupons. Go to matinee performances. Use public transportation to save on parking and fuel. Buy Disney passes from a travel agency before you leave home.

Watch for relevant discount **coupons** in RV magazines and papers picked up on route (at tourist bureaus, park offices, the laundry, etc.).

Check **Camping World** catalogues and flyers for specials before making a purchase. (They don't always tell you.) In the past they have offered free toilet tissue with a $25 purchase. Stock up on holding tank chemicals when they are on sale.

Cut your partner's (and your pet's) **hair**. They say the only difference between a good and bad haircut is two weeks.

Buy an **America the Beautiful pass** (for $80 in 2011) if you will be visiting more than two (U.S.) national parks in the next year. Unfortunately Golden Age passes are not available for Canadians.

Use **e-mail** when possible (probably won't work with your 95 year-old mother).

Use your **phone** company's 800 number when calling Canada, but use coins or a prepaid calling card for in-state or interstate calls. Have a discount plan if you will be using your cellphone a lot. Better yet, use Skype on your computer.

Ask for "**cash back**" with your bank card when shopping at chain stores, rather than using ATM machines with their high transaction fees.

Don't winter in the Florida Keys.

All things considered, RV snowbirds have it pretty easy. Real stress would be traveling the Los Angeles freeway system to and from work each day.

THE RV SNOWBIRD COMMUNITY

They are former doctors, teachers, plumbers, farmers, and sanitation engineers from Halifax, Chicago, Spokane, and White Rock, who in winter head south in a recreational vehicle. When the spirit moves them, they put out the awning, patio mat, and folding chairs and become part of a community probably more closely knit than the one they left behind.

Anthropologist David Counts claims that since the demise of the front porch and sidewalk, the opportunity for casual neighbourhood interaction has all but disappeared. In RV resorts the awning creates a kind of porch, which in turn encourages informal discourse. In suburbia outdoor socializing is occasional backyard barbecues with family and close friends. In a snowbird resort it is frequent happy hours and potluck dinners under the awning with new acquaintances.

Full-Timers and Part-Timers

Full-timers have chosen wheel estate over real estate. In 2011 an estimated three million Americans have disposed of most of their worldly trappings and hit the road in a home-on-wheels. In the winter months the majority hang out in the southern United States or Mexico, and in the summer in the northern states or Canada. In most cases the intention is to return to the real world only when their health interferes with the nomad lifestyle.

Part-timers have a residence other than their rig—"a stick house", where they likely live for the greater part of the year. The restrictions on eligibility for provincial health care (discussed in a later chapter) have discouraged a large number of Canadians from becoming full-timers, but many thousands are part-timers—snowbirds in the winter and Canadians-in-residence during the more friendly months.

Gypsies and Roosters

For the first few years as snowbirds, RVers are often of the traveling variety, exploring Sunbelt America like Charles Kurault with a

Passport America card. As years pass, many get to feeling they've "been there, done that", driving becomes a chore, and they find themselves spending more and more time in one locale, and then at one particular park. At this point they often decide to buy or rent a trailer home in their favourite winter sun spot, or store their rig down south over the summer to use when they return in the winter (also discussed in a later chapter). With dwindling nest eggs to pay high fuel costs many gypsies are becoming roosters sooner than planned.

Roots

The vast majority of snowbirds in the U.S. Sunbelt are from the United States or Canada, although I met a couple in the Western Horizons Rockport laundry, who had had their Mercedes motorhome shipped from Germany. I have noted only one African American couple and no Asians in snowbird RV parks. It seems RVing should be included on the stuffwhitepeoplelike website.

Although most winter RVers are from the United States, a few parks, such as Hot Springs LTVA in southeastern California, have been predominantly Canadian. Our representation would be higher if out-of-country health insurance weren't so restrictive and expensive. The cost of fuel, a previously weak dollar, and low returns on investments have been further deterrents. Predictably, in the western snowbird states and Mexico the largest number of Canadian license plates are from B.C. and Alberta, and in Texas and Florida most are from the eastern provinces. The central provinces go either way.

Partners in Travel (or Not)

An estimated 90% of RV snowbirds travel in pairs. Some of the **singles** have never married, but most are carrying on with a lifestyle they enjoy, after a divorce or death of a spouse. For solo RVers who want companionship and security there are clubs such as the **Blue Jay SINGLES RV Club** in B.C. and the international **RVing Women, Wandering Individuals,** and **Loners on Wheels** (whose t-shirts state *"I've got friends in LoW places").*

To discourage unwanted visitors, one single lady reported leaving a pair of size fourteen boots outside her RV door, and another to putting out a very large bowl and collar on a leash, although she had no dog. The writings of the fearless Sharlene Minshall, adventurous Joei Carlton Hossack (author of *How I Lost 3 Pounds in 30 Years of Dieting Without Going Hungry)*, and *RV gazette* columnist Barbara Cormack are inspirational. Single RVers, especially women, have no trouble attracting help when backing into a site—whether they want it or not.

The **Rainbow RV Club** for gay and lesbian travelers no doubt includes snowbirds.

55 Plus

Many Sunbelt parks have a 55 or older age requirement. As most snowbirds are retirees, this is a problem only for those who exit the workforce early. Letters frequently appear in RV publications from younger folk dreaming of the day when they can become full-timers or at least snowbirds. Many RV snowbirds are in their eighties.

A Classless Society

The financial portfolios of RV snowbirds run the full spectrum. Those with their million dollar coaches, who also own multi-million dollar homes, are often parked next to full-timers in their twenty-year-old trailer—and usually get along just fine.

We met a couple at Pyramid Lake, California, 3000 miles from home in Ontario, traveling with a tent trailer, who were ecstatic at finally being able to take a holiday after decades of hard work. Most long-term RVers have what David Counts calls a **"Zen affluence"**, and live counter to the North American ethic of materialism. Retired RVers rarely talk about their occupation in their previous lives.

The socio-economic mix varies greatly from location to location, clientele at the upscale resorts accepting only motorcoaches no doubt wealthier than those at a $200 a month park in Texas. A surprising number of expensive motorhomes boondock on the Arizona and California deserts, although few at Slab City. Outdoor Resorts of

America and parks in the Florida Keys probably have the highest net worth per capita.

The Typical Snowbird

It was written by Darlene Miller in the September/October, 2003 Escapee magazine:

> *Snowbirds are migratory homo sapiens. . . The crest of the male is quite sparse and usually white to silver gray. However, the female crest and crown may be any shade from white to black, silver to brown, or even yellow or red. They appear to be well-fed to the point that many are plump.*

Their uniform is chosen for comfort rather than style, cotton the fabric of choice. Typical is the T-shirt that reads *"I'm retired. This is as dressed up as I get"*, *"CEO in Charge of Diddly Squat"*, *"Don't Forget My Senior Discount"*, or *"Old Guys Rule!"* RV couples frequently wear matching shirts or jackets. He usually has a cap and she often a wide-brimmed head-covering or visor of some sort. He may have a jump-suit for washing the rig and she a crinoline for square dancing.

Occasionally they stroll the streets in bathrobes, sometimes carrying aqua socks or "noodles"–heading for the shower, pool, or hot tub, where he wears vintage trunks and she a matronly floral suit with tummy control.

Although there is the odd curmudgeon who complains about lights and wind chimes, RV snowbirds are generally more easy-going and friendly than the younger summer campers up north. In a snow-bird park, whether you are driving, walking, biking, or lounging un-der the awning, you will be greeted, or at least given a friendly wave, by virtually everyone.

Snowbird RVers will usually go out of their way to lend a hand. If you want company, simply lift the hood of your truck or motorhome. Paul quickly acquired six assistants in the Club Naples Florida park, looking for the reason our daytime running lights would not shut off. (David Counts cynically attributes this helpfulness, in part, to "not being locked in for life", as one would be in back home.) Close friend-ships frequently develop in Sunbelt parks with long-term seasonal residents.

Snowbirds keep busy–sightseeing, shopping, dancing, golfing, bird watching, walking, hiking, or polishing the rig. They enjoy ca-sinos, bingos, cards, dominoes, billiards, movies, and potluck din-ners. Many work on hobbies which for many years had been on the backburner. Others bask in the luxury of having time to read or do crosswords or Sudokus. An ever-increasing number travel with a computer. The majority are early-to-bed and early-to-rise types, not big on nightlife. On a travel day they like to be on the road before seven.

As indicated by a Sunbelt T-shirt proclaiming: *"Retired, Knows it All, and Has Lots of Time to Tell You About It",* most snowbirds like to talk. Usually that's good, unless they're trying to sell something. Most are knowledgeable on a wide variety of topics: we learned much about sewer hoses, holding tank chemicals, bicycle racks, hitches, destinations, parks, and routes, as well as moose-hunting, quadruple bypasses, and battles of the Second World War. Also about "motor meat"–cooking dinner on the road in your engine compartment!

They have lots of time to tell you about it, and you probably have lots of time to listen. Just don't believe everything you hear via "the Jacuzzi network".

Snowbird Pets

Signs on rigs revealed we have shared parks with "Autry" the "Attack Chihuahua" (pronounced chi-hoo-a-hoo-a by his owner), Miss Murphy, Kola, Duchess, Pumpkin, Oreo, Goliath, and "One Spoiled Dog and its Household Staff". We have also parked near an "Area Patrolled by Dachshund", as well as one "Patrolled by Pomeranian", where we felt particularly safe. At one site was the warning: "Beware of Invisible Dog!!!"

Snowbird dogs come in all shapes, sizes, and breeds. One gentle-man in Deming, New Mexico told me his was a "'kinardly'–you kin 'ardly tell what he is". Short-haired ones are best for easy maintenance in wet weather and comfort in high temperatures. The lapdog variety is good for constricted quarters where, in parked motorhomes, they often become dashboard dogs.

According to many park managers, canines are their biggest **problem**. Not the dogs really, but the masters who don't keep them on a short leash, pick up after them, or prevent them from piddling on tires. Owners forget not everyone is a dog lover. Snowbird dogs are actually much better behaved than the regular campground variety, rarely barking except at a particularly offensive fellow canine or a cyclist. They seem to know they face eviction if deemed a nuisance.

Most Sunbelt resorts accept dogs, although some charge and a large number have size and breed **restrictions**. Many have a separate section for "pet sites", which are often booked a year in advance. Except in Mexico, all parks hand out regulations not to leave your dog unattended, to use a leash, and to "Stoop and Scoop".

It is a big **adjustment** becoming a snowbird dog in the desert. After years of being programmed to piddle on grass, for weeks Simba would look up questioningly when we implored her, "Go pee, Sim", while standing on the packed sand next to the lush green area with the "NO PETS" sign. Some snowbird dogs have collapsible wire yards and some small ones get to cruise around in bicycle baskets. Keep in mind mid-day pavement can be hot on paws.

Many places provide doggie bags and some designate a special washer for pet blankets. Some have official "dog runs" (usually short), but most want you to use "the rough" outside the property for walking and toileting. Be on the lookout for coyotes, snakes, or 'gators, depending on your location. Also for doggie droppings which haven't been picked up.

Some snowbird parks have dog shows and some RV publications have regular pet articles. **Sun-N-Fun's** activity calendar has a "Doggie Memo" column, (at one time) written by canines Chase and Maggie, where it promotes the on-site "Doggy Playpen", but stresses "dogs are not allowed to potty there". (Formidable challenge for the owner.) With Pet City, a grassy treed 2.5 acre area with benches and picnic tables in the center of the resort, as well as a Pet Wash and Annual Pet Parade and Festivities, Yuma's **Cocopah RV and Golf Resort** gets a "10" rating from Autry, Miss Murphy, and Kola.

Pet City, Cocopah Golf and RV Resort

Because of their fastidious grooming and toileting habits and inde-pendent nature, in many ways **cats** are ideal snowbird pets, although I have seen few looking comfortable on a leash, as required when out-side by park regulations. Because they also like to explore and curl up in small spaces, always check your cat's whereabouts before opening the door and operating the slideout. Felines, too, like to bask in the sun on dashboards, as well as on tables next to windows.

In semitropical locations pets seriously affect your **lifestyle.** Small well-behaved ones can often be taken into stores in snugglies or canvas bags, but only pet stores and Camping World welcome them. A few large entertainment venues like Disney parks offer on-site **kennels,** but they are not common and there never seem to be private options nearby. There are of course long-term boarding facilities and veterinarians will often take pets for the day. For short periods they can stay in the rig with the air conditioner or Fan-Tastic Fan. The restraints placed on outings deters many RVers from getting or replacing a dog or cat.

Travelling pets need bedding, toys, medical records, and some-times medication. Snowbird pets are extremely pampered. To empty-nesters they are their children and often influence the choice of winter residence.

Snowbird Rigs

In membership parks the majority of motorhomes are Class A's—mainly Fleetwood or Winnebago/Itasca models, although there are also a fair number of high-end Allegros and Mountain Aires. As you gaze enviously at the half-million dollar coaches, realize that their owners are most likely full-timers and this is their full-time home. Rigs with Canadian plates are generally more modest, as few from that country are full-time RVers.

Fifth wheels are very popular in Arizona and California, but not so much in Florida, I guess because there are few "truck people" in the eastern part of America. Regular trailers are more common in non-membership parks. Almost all trailers, except for the most expensive fifth wheels, are white.

Snowbird RV's often have bumper stickers such as *"We're Spending Our Children's Inheritance"* or *"We're Not Old. We're Recycled Teenagers".*

RV Snowbird Paraphernalia

To be a bona fide member of the RVing snowbird community you gotta have certain stuff.

Give yourself points for hydraulic levelers, tire covers, window awnings, a solar screen for the front window, covers for windshield wipers and mirrors, Patty O'Shades or screen rooms, and for each slideout and solar panel. As virtually all Sunbelt RV's have air conditioners and awnings over the patio, no points for them.

Real snowbirds have cellphones, computers, satellite dishes, padded recliners, barbecue grills, bikes (often with a basket, no gears, and golf ball on the kickstand), golf clubs, and often pool noodles, pool cues, and California dusters.

Their RV's are adorned with dashboard animals (real or stuffed), hanging wire fruit baskets (or bags), ladders, and sometimes wooden name signs. Jugs of purified water weighting down the satellite dish and polypropylene patio rug (which probably matches the awning) complete the image. Points for each of the above.

Bonuses for colour-coordinated towed and towing vehicle, extra shine on the rig, and a horn that plays "On the Road Again" or "Merrily We Roll Along".

Snowbird ratings: 20+ - whooping crane
15-19 - pelican
8-14 - roadrunner
7 and under - cactus wren

We were roadrunners.

Do It All or Nothing At All

You can do it all, or nothing at all. As on cruise ships, so it is too in RV snowbird megaresorts, some of which promote themselves as a place "Where the Fun Never Sets".

Instead of lobster and filet mignon RV snowbirds dine on potluck and hobo stew. Instead of tiramisu and crème brulé there are root beer floats and donuts. In place of gaming in the casinos there is penny poker in the rec hall. In lieu of Vegas-style shows and orchestras there are jam sessions, karaoke, and Don the DJ. Thousand dollar bingo jackpots in the Masquerade Theatre differ somewhat from nickel-a-card bonanzas in the clubhouse, but, as on The Love Boat, there are lots of activity choices and a usually a social director to guide you.

Even the most basic snowbird park has a clubhouse, swimming pool, book exchange, and at least one billiard table. A large number offer mini-golf, horseshoe pits, shuffleboard, bocce and pickle ball courts, ballrooms, exercise rooms, card rooms, and facilities for silversmith, lapidary, ceramics, stained glass making, and woodworking. Some have ping pong tables, tennis courts, softball diamonds, lap pools, computer labs, and par 3 golf courses. A few have batting cages and golf driving cages.

You will find square dancing at almost any RV park in southern Texas, Spanish classes at many parks near the Mexican border, and fishing at parks on water—salt, inland, or manmade (common in Florida). Individual resorts have their own specialties, based on the interests of returning snowbirds. Siesta Bay in Fort Myers has a camera club, Royal Coachman near Sarasota a train club, Valle del Oro near Phoenix motorcycle and remote-controlled airplane clubs, and Voyager RV Resort east of Tucson offers astronomy, barbershop singing, and clowning. At least they did at one time.

Many snowbird resorts organize inter-park bowling leagues, pool and golf tournaments, shopping and sightseeing tours, casino trips, and talent shows. Some require residents to wear badges to distinguish them from interlopers.

Fun in the Sun

From the activity schedule presented at check-in, a typical day at Sarasota's 1600-site **Sun-N-Fun Resort** includes: lap swim, morning coffee, computer lab, low impact aerobics, mat exercises, aqua hydra fit, aqua aerobics, hatha yoga, volleyball, mixed doubles tennis, lawn bowling, petanque, horseshoes, Texas horseshoes, bowling pin shuffle board, newcomers' shuffle, 15 cent shuffle, billiards, golf, stained glass (beginners), lapidary, woodworking, quilting, one-stroke painting, sailboat racing, ham radio, 5 and 10 cent poker, pinochle partners, duplicate bridge, Sun-N-Fun chorus, line, round, and square dancing (also lessons).

That's Monday. Other days also schedule blood pressure testing, bingo, book club, bridge lessons, party bridge, euchre, water color painting, decorative painting, tatting, chime classes, ceramics, shirt appliqué, mohair teddy bear classes, bocce ball, bible study, crocheting, "greedy dice", piano/organ practice, mountain dulcimer, yoga for golfers, and Reiki Healing.

March's calendar noted: church services, brunch, and live entertainment poolside on Sundays; ESPN Sports Night on Mondays; karaoke poolside on Tuesdays and Fridays; barbecue dinners, newcomer potluck, St Patrick's Day Blast, and game night on the Wednesdays; bingo on Thursdays; dances, plus a magic show, the Stage Door Players, an SNF variety show, and a Year End Beach Party on the Saturdays.

Or you can watch Dr. Phil or read Grisham in the rig.

Let's Get Physical

With no snow to shovel, grass to mow, or decks to paint, it would seem snowbirds are doomed to pack on pounds, but most establish an exercise regime. Walkers are often out by 7 am, in desert locations usually garbed in jackets and long pants and sometimes gloves and toques. Early bird doggies often wear sweaters. Nordic walking (with poles) is gaining in popularity.

Many parks have scheduled morning **walking** groups around the resort or its environs, and some, notably in Yuma and nearby

Foothills, organize major hikes to which you drive and sometimes stay overnight. Geo-caching (described below) adds a new dimension to hiking.

Golfers usually choose an early tee time over a five-course breakfast, with trips to the links often organized by the RV park. (I read recently: "Golf is a game where you yell 'fore!', shoot six, and write down five.")

At 7 am serious **swimmers** will not have to contend with width-walkers, games of Marco Polo, or the "soaker", who wants to talk at length about her lazy son-in-law or precocious grandchildren. At dawn the temperature of the pool is considerably warmer than the air.

Later in the day there are water **aerobics**, usually with a perky instructor and golden oldies music. Low-impact aerobics, chair exercises, Pilates, and tai chi are also common in snowbird parks, some of which have weights and cardio equipment (of varying quality). Washing and polishing the rig also provide an upper body and cardio workout.

Polishing the rig (note the flag)

At Hemet's Golden Village Palms you can dance from morning to night. Desert Hot Springs' Catalina RV Resort has daily beginning, intermediate, and advanced line **dancing**, whose popularity I figure has much to do with not needing a partner. Clogging is popular at Cocopah RV Resort in Yuma, ballroom dancing in the Mesa megaresorts, and, as previously mentioned, square dancing anywhere in southern Texas. Some parks have tap dancing sessions.

Or you can boogie in the rig with Richard Simmons (exercise videos).

Let the Games Begin (title of Sun-N-Fun's Activity Program)

In addition to golf, horseshoes, shuffleboard, lawn bowling, billiards, pickle ball, and bocce ball, many snowbirds are into snake toss and bean bag toss.   If there isn't a bingo game in progress in the clubhouse, you will likely find tables of bridge, euchre, po-ke-no, dominoes (often Mexican Train), Scrabble, Pegs and Jokers, and/or cribbage. (I don't know if "Hand and Foot" requires a table.) Some locations have official "card rooms".

No self-respecting RV park is complete without a jigsaw puzzle or two on the go—in the clubhouse, library, and/or laundry.

Geo-Caching

Geo-caching is a treasure hunt requiring Internet access and a handheld global positioning apparatus, initiated by typing in your local zip code at the geocaching.com website to get a list of nearby geocache locations, their co-ordinates, and a few clues.

The sites, always on public lands, are rated with one to five stars, according to the difficulty of locating the "cache", usually a sealed plastic container filled with trinkets—from which you "take one and leave one". Also inside are a log book and pencil to record your arrival.

Often hidden in scenic locations, reaching the treasure requires varying degrees of physical output, in addition to GPS skills and visual acuity. Promoted by Tom and Stephanie Gonser on their rversonline. org website and at RV conferences, the "techno-sport" is well-suited for RVers, many of whom like to hike.

"Wood Butchers" and "Crafty Ladies"

–are found at Encore's Harlingen RV Resort and Casa Grande's Sundance I RV Resort, respectively. Large parks offer every conceivable craft–beading, sewing, crocheting, quilting, painting, basket weaving, leather tooling, ceramics, woodworking, silversmithing, lapidary, macramé, rubber stamps, and on and on. If they don't have your specialty, the activity director would probably love to enlist you as an organizer/instructor. Park swap meets, craft fairs, and patio sales provide opportunities to sell your handiwork.

Tours and Tag-Alongs

At RV parks near casinos there are often bus trips to the gaming establishments, which lure patrons with free buffets, gaming vouchers, or sometimes cash. Non-gamblers can enjoy the impressive hotels, free shows, and people-watching.

At parks in and around big cities, Grey Line Tours will be glad to show you the sights. Common in smaller parks are "tag-alongs", where interested parties meet at the clubhouse and then head off together, on foot or in vehicles, to local restaurants, attractions, or golf courses.

No Formal Nights

Snowbird parks are known for their icecream socials, potluck dinners, and barbecues, which offer a change from your regular menu and dinner companion. Sometimes there is an onsite restaurant, with a limited menu and hours, or at least a basic kitchen, offering one or two dishes for breakfast, lunch, and/or dinner, where interested parties sign up in advance and bring their own plates and cutlery.

Dinner at the clubhouse

Pancakes, biscuits and gravy, hotdogs, hamburgers, and barbecued chicken or steak are common menu items. (Waffles in the shape of the Lone Star State were the high point of our free breakfast at Gulf Coast RV Park in Beaumont, Texas.) Hobo stew, where everyone contributes a can of vegetables, is also popular. Most park dinners start at five o'clock, with no second sitting. The cruise ship analogy does not apply to snowbird resort dining!

Dinner parties at the rig are low-key affairs—usually outside, with mismatched dishes or Styrofoam plates and plastic glasses. No Royal Doulton china, crystal goblets, or linen napkins folded into swans. Usually everyone brings a dish and sometimes their own place setting. Boondockers have been known to cook "trashcan turkey" for Thanksgiving and Christmas.

Most snowbirds are frugal when it comes to dining out, the majority preferring to "do lunch". An Internet posting tells of a young pupil who reported that when his grandparents (who lived in a "tin box" in Arizona) went out for dinner they always had "early birds", but usually they ate in the "wrecked center".

But No Carmel Lattes

Many snowbird parks offer early morning coffee to greet the day and provide an opportunity to mingle with fellow-RVers. At our stay at Pioneer Beach RV Resort in Port Aransas, Texas it was available from 5 am! Often muffins or cinnamon buns can be purchased for a nominal amount. Coffee and free donuts are usually included at onsite RV brake and safety seminars and RV dealership displays later in the day.

Happy Hour

Groups of four to ten happy people often congregate at predetermined rigs from 4 to 5pm, equipped with folding chairs and liquid refreshments, and sit around and tell lies. Some snowbird parks also schedule Friday happy hours at the clubhouse or around the pool, where you bring your own drinks and munchies for the group.

Finally Time to Read

Even the most modest RV park has an informal book exchange where you can borrow or "bring one and take one", and the laundry always has magazines, although usually a couple of years old. Desert Shadows RV Resort in Casa Grande has an official library with over 3500 books which you sign out, as well as a volunteer librarian. Book swaps are ideal for traveling bookworms who begrudge valuable storage space when they are finished a book. Second-hand bookstores and flea markets are also good sources for cheap reads.

If you will be staying in one location for a month or so, local libraries will often let you take out books if you have proof of (even short-term) residency, which can be obtained by mailing yourself an envelope or postcard to your park address. Public libraries also offer Internet use, classes, presentations, and a wealth of information on the surrounding area.

Electronic books (such as Kindle) are another option to carrying around bulky paper ones.

Snowbirds Online

Nowadays most snowbirds use e-mail as the main means of keeping in touch with the folks back home. With the demise of Pocketmail, more and more are travelling with a laptop computer where they can also use the Net to get information on news, weather, destinations, parks, or anything else from "aardvark" to "zymurgy". Many use **social networking sites** to document their travels, often with pictures.

A free **Skype** Internet download with a headset will transform a computer into a telephone, and with a webcam will add video. To other computers with Skype the service is free and to land lines and cellphones the cost is a few cents a minute.

Virtually all privately operated parks offer Internet service and more and more have **wi-fi**, where RVers can Google in the comfort of their rig–usually for a fee. Many public libraries and travel plazas and all Texas interstate rest stops offer free wireless access from their parking areas. Use the wififreespot.com website to learn about free locations, but don't do sensitive transactions in public venues because of possible hackers.

Of the numerous websites for RVers, rversonline.org, rvadvice. com, and freetrip.com are particularly valuable. The first follows the extensive travels of Tom and Stephanie Gonser presented in Stephanie's entertaining style, as well as provides up-to-date information important to RVers.

Church Services

Most snowbird parks have a Sunday non-denominational service and some offer bible study and choir groups.

Not Dreaming of a White Christmas

Yes, Virginia, there is still Christmas without snow. Many RVers decorate their rigs and in non-windy locations some set up a Christmas tree outside. Camping World has special RV Christmas cards. Snowbird parks organize holiday crafts, dances, dinners, entertainment, tree-trimming, carol-singing, and church services. You will miss family and friends back home, but probably not the cooking and dishes for twenty. When you phone with season's greetings, realize it would be mean-spirited to discuss the weather.

The life of an RV snowbird depends on the park and the individual. Some, like me, are happiest camping in the desert, in a wilderness site overlooking a lake, or, best of all, right on the water–reading, writing, and biking. Others, like Paul, need hook-ups and people (and in his case also a pool table and nearby Chinese restaurant). Most snowbirds experience a combination of the two worlds. At least in the beginning, until they find that perfect home away from home.

To quote Shirley Slate and Harry Bosch in *Freewheelin' USA*: "It's your dream. You call the shots."

SOUTHERN CALIFORNIA—FOR HOT SPRINGS, CASINOS, AND SLAB CITY

With its southern border further north than all of Florida, California would seem at a geographical disadvantage as a snowbird destination. Also, a large section of the southern part of the state is taken up with the inhospitable Mojave Desert, and the coastal regions, so popular in the summer, are cool and rainy during the winter months.

Only the land south of I-40 has temperatures suitable for winter RV living, but that's plenty of space for the hundreds of thousands of snowbird rigs heading to Palm Springs and its bedroom communities, to the banks of the Colorado River, to the desert lands in the southeast corner of the state, and to the area referred to as the Inland Empire. Locations where daytime temperatures rarely dip below 70.

Sunbelt California rivals Arizona for cloudless skies. Humidity is not an issue as in Florida. In spite of desert winds and cool overnight temperatures, there are lots of opportunities to be out there havin' fun in the warm California sun.

Hiking is popular along the Colorado River, in Joshua Tree National Park, in Anza-Borrego and Perris Lake State Parks, in the Indian Canyons near Palm Springs, and in the San Jacinto Wilderness Area. **Rock climbers** love the tumbled wonderland of bizarre boulders in Joshua Tree National Park. **ATV buffs** are drawn to the Algodones Dune Area south of I-8 (off-roading is not allowed on the north side).

The Salton Sea Wildlife Refuge, on the Pacific Fly Route, is a **bird-watcher**'s paradise. **Fishing** and **boating** are also popular on The Sea (actually a lake), as well as on Perris Lake and the Colorado River.

Greater Palm Springs has over 100 beautifully manicured **golf** courses with mountain backdrops. Many of the links are open to the public, who can save up to 60% (on prices up to $300 a round) by contacting Next Day Golf at 760 345-8463 or Stand-by Golf at 760 321-2665. Duffers on a budget can play at the nearby par 3 Desert Crest course, the Sands RV and Golf Resort in Desert Hot Springs, the Indio municipal par 3, or the full-size Ivey Ranch course in Thousand Palms. The area hosts celebrity golf and professional tennis tournaments, including the Pacific Life Open at the Indian Wells Tennis Garden in March.

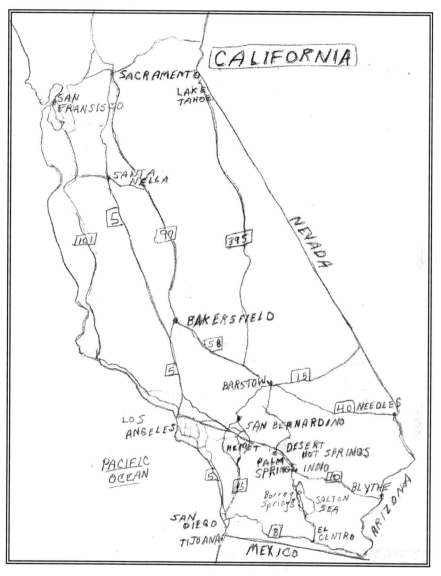

Map of Southern California

Hot mineral waters, in and around Desert Hot Springs (whose spas attract Hollywood elite), in the area east of the Salton Sea, and in Holtville (east of El Centro), offer therapeutic benefits.

With six major **casinos** on native lands in and near Palm Springs, the area has the highest concentration of gaming outlets of the major snowbird destinations—only Vegas, Reno, Laughlin, and Biloxi (Mississippi) with more.

Shopping is also centered in the Palm Springs area, with exclusive shops, upscale malls, swap meets, and street fairs (notably the weekly Village Fest on Palm Canyon Drive and the weekend event at the College of the Desert). Catering to the locals, but worth a look, is the Indio open-air market at the fairgrounds—offering everything from jalapenos to beds to bras. The Cabazon Outlet Stores are a few miles west on I-10. There is a Trader Joe's outlet. Art lovers will enjoy the **galleries** and special exhibits on El Paseo Drive.

One to two hours west of California's snowbird hotspots are **Los Angeles** and **San Diego**, with the ocean, theme parks, sporting events, and many shopping and cultural opportunities. Both cities are embarkation points for cruises to Hawaii, Mexico, and the Panama Canal—good deals, including transportation to and from the dock, advertised in local papers. Travel agencies also offer packages for audience participation in television shows filmed in LA and Hollywood. Best to leave the rig in the RV park when you tackle southern California's infamous freeways to visit west coast attractions.

On the downside, prices in southern California for accommodations (including campgrounds), food, and fuel are consistently among the nation's highest.

Campgrounds

RV parks in Sunbelt California run the gamut from the exclusive Outdoor Resort Indio near Palm Springs to the unique Slab City near the Salton Sea. There are few full-time retirement/snowbird parks compared with Texas and Florida, but avoid ones which include "Mobile Home Park" or "Residential Park" in their names. California has the most membership parks of the Sunbelt states.

With its attractive desert setting encircled by milk chocolate coloured mountains and liberally garnished with palms and splotches of green, an abundance of amenities, and proximity to the coast, the **Palm Springs** area is California's prime wintering ground. Most of the RV resorts are out of the high-rent district, in nearby Desert Hot Springs and Indio.

January to March Western Horizons' Desert Pools and Indian Waters parks are difficult to access and the Thousand Trails park operates at capacity, but Coast to Coast's/ RPI's Catalina Spa and Resort usually has space. Of the non-membership parks, those in the Palm Springs area charge over $1000 a month, and on the other side of I-10, Caliente Springs is the most expensive, at around $600. Owners of Newells and American Eagles should head for one of the Outdoor Resorts locations or the Emerald Desert Golf and RV Resort in Palm Desert, exclusive parks with rates upwards of $1500 a month (plus pet charges in some cases).

Our favourite site at Indian Waters RV Resort, Indio

On the east side of the **Salton Sea** (one of the world's largest inland bodies of salt water and California's largest lake) are the Fountain of Youth Spa and RV Resort with 930 sites, and the smaller lower-priced Imperial Spa and Bashfords Hot Mineral Spa. Because of dead fish and birds, the lakefront Salton Sea State Recreation area with 165 sites (some hook-ups) attracts few RVers. There is always room (but no hook-ups) at the incomparable Slab City near Niland, discussed later in the chapter.

There are a number of RV parks along the **Colorado River,** including CRA locations at Needles and Earp, Big River RV Resort, and the Imperial Dam Long Term Visitors Area for wilderness campers.

The government operates **LTVA**'s on the open desert lands in the southeast corner of the state, where campers can hang out for $180 for seven months or $40 for two weeks. They may also stay for free on the desert outside of an LTVA for up to 14 days, after which time they must move to a new location outside a 25-mile radius from the original spot.

The **Anza-Borrego** area offers scenic desert camping (some on government lands) near the charming town of Borrego Springs (where we witnessed a bank robbery in 2001!). **El Centro,** near the Mexican border, is also a popular reasonably-priced RV winter destination and there is a Sunbelt USA park at **Pilot Knob,** surrounded by well-used public lands, a few miles west of Yuma, Arizona—hard to get into in peak time.

Although the sun is not as reliable on the other side of the mountains, many RV snowbirds choose the pastoral countryside around **Hemet, Temecula,** or **Perris,** Hemet's 1041-site Golden Village Palms (the state's largest) regularly advertising special rates (800 394-2226) in RV publications. The Prevost crowd will prefer Outdoor Resorts Rancho California, 18 miles east of Temecula. RVers should avoid taking the rig on the steep winding mountain **Highway 74,** the most direct route between Palm Springs and the so-called Inland Empire.

Palm Springs—Jewel of the Desert

Leaving the interstate at the "Palm Springs" exit you find yourself on a two-lane road heading into the desert with thousands of wind turbines and signs warning of "Blowing Sand", but for several miles no indication of the legendary Playground of the Stars.

An unpretentious community huddled at the foot of 10,000' Mt. San Jacinto, Palm Springs sprung out of wasteland like Las Vegas, but is much more subdued and tasteful. In place of theme-park-style mega-hotels embellished with neon, glitz, and slot machines, the Palm Springs area has elegant, low-rise, five-star hotels in beautiful golf course settings. There are casinos and one-armed bandits, but not in every hotel, restaurant, and washroom, as in Vegas.

Locals call it "**The Strip**", but with several blocks of modest two-story hotels (only the Hilton is higher), motels, restaurants, shops, and businesses, downtown Palm Canyon Drive is the antithesis of Las Vegas Boulevard. The single gaming facility actually in the city is two blocks off The Strip, and the only chorus girls are the 50-to 80- year old long-stemmed lovelies in "**The Fabulous Palm Springs Follies**". The area's casinos host big-name entertainers, although not Celine Dion or Wayne Newton.

Greater Palm Springs stretches thirty-five miles east down the Coachella Valley, encompassing eight distinctive communities, of which Rancho Mirage is the most affluent and Indio the most Hispanic and blue collar. A commonality is the multitude of golf courses which checker the Valley, most hidden behind formidable walls and high hedges.

There are a number of upscale steakhouses and seafood **restaurants** catering to celebrities and well-heeled tourists, but there are also reasonably-priced buffets, Mexican and Chinese eateries, fast food outlets, and the ubiquitous Outback Steakhouse and Olive Garden for the rest of us.

With less glamour, **Desert Hot Springs** has few golf courses, expensive homes, and greenbelts, and no fancy restaurants or high-class shopping outlets, but it has the same mountains and reliable sunshine as across the freeway—as well as world-renowned therapeutic springs and affordable RV parks. (Plus a little more wind!)

The 8500' rotating **Palm Springs Aerial Tramway** up Mt. San Jacinto offers a magnificent view as well as cooler temperatures and 80 km of hiking trails at the summit. Other local attractions include the **Indian Canyons**, the Palm Springs **Desert Museum**, the 1200 acre **Living Desert Zoo and Gardens**, and the Palm Springs **Windmill Tour**, the world's only exhibit of a working wind farm. (None have kennels.)

Living Desert Zoo and Gardens

The scenic **Palms to Pines Highway** (Highway 74 which rises from 400' to 4000') and **Anza Borrego** and **Joshua Tree National Parks** are popular day trips.

The Southeast Corner–The *Real* Desert

Turning south from Indio, onto Highway 86 or the newer faster 86S, orchards of date trees replace the Coachella golf courses, and eventually give way to bona-fida desert lands.

Although it has much lower prices and less rain than Palm Springs an hour or so away, except for a loyal clientele at the Fountain of Youth Spa and RV Resort, relatively few snowbirds are drawn to the area around the **Salton Sea**. In the 1950's heralded as a destination to rival Palm Springs, tourist establishments opened and the lake was stocked with fish, but the high salt content and run-off of farmland pesticides killed much of the marine life and many of the birds drawn to the large body of water.

There is still fishing (don't eat the catch) and bird watching is good, but few facilities remain. A restoration process, spearheaded by former Palm Springs' mayor Sonny Bono, is underway to improve the water, curb the death rate of wildlife, and revive the abandoned resort communities and waterfront state campground. For now the area is brown and unappealing.

However, RVers traveling past The Sea to points south, should take a side trip to **Slab City** on the east side—a dismantled military base, whose concrete foundations, parking areas, and remnants of paved streets are the basis of an RV gathering place for full-time squatters and boondocking snowbirds, including some pretty eccentric characters. Many residents work in town and some two dozen students are bussed to school. Located a few miles east of Niland, you can't miss the entrance with its vividly painted Salvation Mountain (constructed of hay bales and hundreds of gallons of recycled paint) and brightly decorated pickup truck with a small church in the truck box.

Salvation Mountain, Slab City

Camping is free, although there is a charge for water delivery and honey wagon service. (Most visitors dig "gopher holes" for waste disposal and some long-term residents install rudimentary septic systems.) There are view sites on the ridge, groves of trees, and no pet rules. There is a clubhouse (an old trailer) where they hold dances, potlucks, and games. There are also weekend "garage" sales and "gravel golf"! It has been called "a birdwatcher's dream of heaven", and "the flagship of boondocking sites". For years there have been rumours it will be closed down but for now Slab City, subject of a recent TV documentary, lives on.

Continuing down Highway 111 you reach El Centro and then Mexico. Turn east on I-8 and you come to the Algodones Dune Area (location of several film productions including Star Wars) and the popular **public lands** operated by the Bureau of Land Management of Southern California described above.

The Inland Empire–Link with the Real World

Turning south off I-10 at Beaumont the grey desert is overtaken by grassy areas, punctuated with trees, cattle, and masses of oddly-shaped hills, many speckled with boulders. The sky is not the cerulean blue you get day after day to the northeast. Sometimes there are clouds and occasionally even rain, but there is also less wind.

Hemet is a typical snowbird town in this atypical Southern California setting. The several reasonably-priced RV resorts (notably Golden Village Palms), with all the requisite bells and whistles, plus lively inter-park billiard and shuffleboard leagues, attract repeat long-term winter visitors, including many Canadians.

On a weekday in the non-hookup section of **Lake Perris** State Recreation Area your only neighbours are gophers, rabbits, and chipmunks, and the few boats on the lake and occasional car in the day use area below are the only signs of civilization. On weekends the ambience changes with the arrival of young couples with tents and sleeping bags and teenagers with beer and ghetto blasters.

In the hook-up area the sites are half the size, twice as expensive, and on the weekend filled with families escaping the cities. In place of the gophers, rabbits, and chipmunks, we had Sean, Debbie, Michael, Rachel, and Charlie the Dog in their camper, which had been given to them by a friend, a disgruntled woman who did not want her soon-to-be ex-husband to have it. It was the first time in months we had spent more than five minutes with anyone under fifty and we were pleased we were still able to communicate.

It was also refreshing to hang out in the non-snowbird town of Perris. We were usually the oldest at the $4.99 Chinese buffet Paul dragged me to twice (once on Valentine's Day!). I enjoyed helping a high school girl in the Perris library locate a book on poetry writing. Teenagers in bare feet roamed the aisles in Stater Brothers. The booths in Burger King were filled with chattering young 'uns.

California's Inland Empire, a cross between Palm Springs and Slab City on the budget and reality scales, is a good transition zone for your return to the real world.

Check out visitcalifornia.com or phone 800 862-2543 for further information on the Golden State.

Arizona–for Cacti, Quartzsite, and The Colorado River

Best known for the Grand Canyon, to quote the AAA state tour book, "Arizona is more than simply gorges". To many it is the #1 Snowbird State. Its golf courses are as impressive, shopping as extensive, and recreational opportunities as diverse as in Florida and California. It has the proximity to Mexico and colourful history of Texas. Its scenery and weather are unrivalled. And it's a dry heat–rain in the Phoenix weather forecast cause for great excitement.

Arizona has over 300 **golf** courses, many in spectacular settings, designed by the world's top link architects and used for PGA and LPGA tournaments. Greater Phoenix claims about half the courses and is recognized as one of the top five golf destinations in the world. But watch for Gila monsters, scorpions, and rattlesnakes in the rough.

Hiking opportunities are as varied as the state itself and Arizona's imposing rock formations have given birth to the sport of "canyoneering". Serious hikers should get Scott Warren's *100 Hikes in Arizona*, not all of which are accessible in the winter (snowbird) months. A hat, sunscreen, sturdy shoes, and lots of water are necessities for those exploring canyon floors and desert regions. Many Arizona hikers are rockhounds. Again, be on the lookout for critters in the underbrush. Mountain **biking** is also popular.

The Colorado River–Arizona's "West Coast"–offers all types of boating, as well as rafting, fishing, waterskiing, jetskiing, swimming, and in many locations a beach-like ambience. In a state with few water features, The Colorado is more highly esteemed than the Amazon, Nile, or Danube. Lake Powell and Lake Havasu, wide parts of the River formed by Glen Canyon and Parker Dams respectively, are tourist hotspots. **Wildlife refuges** along the Colorado are home to birds, beavers, raccoons, bighorn sheep, and coyotes.

The Sonoran Desert, which encompasses the southern half of the state, has over 2500 types of flowering plants, more than 300 species of birds, and 100 varieties of cacti. Drives through Organ Pipe Cactus National Monument and Saguaro National Parks are awe-inspiring.

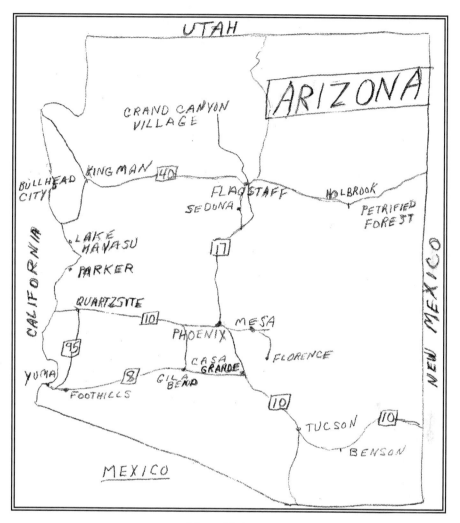

Map of Arizona

The Arizona Living Desert west of Tucson showcases more than 300 animal species and over 1300 plants indigenous to the Sonoran Desert, in their natural habitats along two miles of pathways. Boyce Arboretum State Park east of Phoenix also exhibits an extensive garden of desert plants and trees, as well as birds native to the arid regions of the world.

The **Grand Canyon**, with each stratum of rock marking a period of the earth's history from 2 billion to 250 million years ago, will be of special interest to archaeologists and geologists. **Rockhounds** should not miss Quartzsite's Rock and Gem show the end of January and/ or beginning of February. **Cavers** must visit the Kartchner Caverns east of Tucson. **Dig sites** at Eldon Pueblo, a Hopi ancestral area near Flagstaff, and Old Pueblo, a Hohokam village near Tucson, welcome amateurs.

For **history** buffs there are Wupatki and Walnut Canyon Monuments with ruins of cliff-dwellers, the Casa Grande Ruins, Yuma Territorial Prison, various Civil War battlefields, Tombstone, and other Wild West sites, plus many historical museums throughout the state. The longest remaining stretch of **Route 66**, the first paved transcontinental highway, can be followed between Ashfork and Needles on the California border, with Kingman the most noteworthy stop. Visitor bureaus have books on *The Mother Road,* as well as brochures on Arizona ghost towns.

For **astronomers** there are several observatories within 80 miles of Tucson—in areas of high peaks, clear dry air, and no city lights. Kitt Peak and Whipple offer tours. Pluto (although now delisted as a planet) was discovered at Lowell Observatory in Flagstaff.

For **sports** fans Phoenix has NHL, NFL, NBA, and big league baseball teams with spring training camps; horse, greyhound, and Indy racing; and golf and tennis tournaments.

The Grand Canyon State is a **shopper's** paradise, with the upscale boutiques of Scottsdale; the outlet malls of Casa Grande and Tempe (the state's largest); Junkmarts in Phoenix, Mesa, and Apache Junction; and the quintessential winter garage sale at Quartzsite. Specialty shops and roadside stands offer Native American handicrafts such as silver and turquoise jewelry, woven rugs, baskets, and Kachina dolls. Neighbouring Mexico extends the choices.

There are a number of small **casinos** on Indian lands throughout the state, as well as low-cost junkets to Las Vegas and Laughlin in Nevada from many of the RV parks in the west-central area.

Campgrounds

Most of Arizona's RV snowbird roosts are clustered in Mesa and Apache Junction east of Phoenix, along the Colorado River (notably in Yuma and Lake Havasu), in and around Casa Grande and Tucson, and on the BLM Lands in the southwest corner of the state, with rates decreasing with distance from the cities. Higher in altitude, Arizona's northern half is too cold for snowbirds.

Although some RV communities have full-time residents and many have a 55+ age requirement, there are few "retirement parks", common in Florida and southern Texas, which simply fill in vacant spots with snowbirds. Many southern Arizona RV parks close in the summer because of scorching temperatures. Most resorts in the cities are made up largely of park models, although a few, like Meridian RV Resort in Mesa, are "For RV's Only".

There are a number of parks associated with Western Horizons, Colorado River Adventures, and Thousand Trails (mostly ELS properties). An increasing number of Arizona resorts are selling home park **memberships** and/or lots.

More appealing to many (but not those wanting amenities) are smaller, government, and wilderness parks.

Tens of thousands of snowbirds flock to the **BLM lands** between Quartzsite and Yuma, even from the eastern provinces and states and many in luxury coaches. Some desert areas are free if you move at least 25 miles every two weeks, but for many desert camping is not a matter of economics. (See the chapter on Nesting Sites and One Night Stands.)

Arizona also has a number of reasonably-priced **state-operated campgrounds**, many located at historic or tourist locations, all with fresh water and a dump station, and some with electricity. (The parks at Picacho Peak and Lake Havasu are personally recommended.) Reservations are not taken and at most there is a 15 day limit. There is also a collection of campgrounds (with a total of 533 sites) in the Tonto National Forest area east of Phoenix where you can enjoy boating and fishing and stay up to six months.

The "West Coast"

Bullhead City began in the 1940's as a construction town for the Davis Dam. Today its main attraction is proximity to Little Las Vegas (**Laughlin**) across the Colorado River. At one time most of the

Laughlin hotels offered free dry camping, but are now required to charge and install hook-ups for RV overnighting. Many snowbirds choose the parks in Bullhead City and take the ferry across the River to the action. Surprisingly, Bullhead does not have a CRA resort, although there is a well-used Coast to Coast facility.

Once a former motor-testing site in the middle of the desert, **Lake Havasu City** was put on the map in 1963 when the original London Bridge (one of the world's largest antiques) was transported there, brick by brick, followed by construction of an adjacent English village with British-style shops and eateries. It is a clean modern city with good shopping, dining, and recreational facilities, lots of greenery (although few residential lawns), two nearby wildlife refuges, and a low crime rate. Its location on the Colorado River encourages water sports of all kinds. We noted a great expansion in the eight years between visits, as well as a huge increase in traffic.

London Bridge, Lake Havasu City

With an actual lake (really a 45-mile long wide spot in the River), predictably Lake Havasu RV sites are among the most expensive in the state and in peak periods there is usually a shortage. The CRA park is impossible to get into unless you are a member. The Islander RV Park, which advertises itself as "Arizona's Most Highly Rated Waterfront Resort" in 2011 has rates close to $500 a week. Crazy Horse and Beachcomber are more reasonable. Sites in the state park, with no hook-ups or reservations, are often available before noon.

Parker is of interest to snowbirds because it is on the Colorado in sunny Arizona, and for CRA members there is inexpensive accommodation across the "big reddish green river" (as described in an *RV Times* submission) in Earp, California. Other RV parks line the River between Parker and Lake Havasu, Buckskin Mountain State Park among the most appealing. Parker Dam, the deepest in the world, with 73% of its 320 feet below the original riverbed, can be visited with a self-guided tour.

Yuma

Arizona's third largest city has the greatest proportion of Canadians of any major RV snowbird destination. With over 20% of Yuma's 100,000+ winter visitors from Canada, its *Sun Visitor* newspaper, in addition to sections on "The Desert Snowbird" and "Park Events", devotes half a page to "The Canadian Scene". The surrounding irrigated agricultural land, a relief from the great expanse of desert, is somewhat reminiscent of B.C.'s Fraser Valley farmland. Distant mountains and mesas complement the bucolic setting. The nearby wilderness areas attract large numbers of rockhounds and hiking groups, which form in virtually every area RV park.

Yuma offers all the requisite shopping, dining, and medical facilities of a city, without the higher prices, pollution, crime, and traffic problems of Phoenix. Many snowbirds take courses and check e-mail at the community college and shop at the Phoenix-calibre Yuma Palms Mall. Clear air and low humidity contribute to the Sunbelt's most delightful climate, with average winter temperatures 4 to 5 degrees warmer than the state capital's (appreciated after the sun sets). The Farmer's Almanac claims Yuma has the best weather in the United States (although it can be windy), and it has been named by *Money* magazine as one of the best places in the country to live. It is also recognized as "The Lettuce Capital of the United States".

Reasonably-priced RV parks are the main appeal for budget-conscious Canadians, who have a choice of more than 80 campgrounds, many in the less expensive Foothills area to the east. Most of Yuma's snowbirds come for the winter and stay in the same park every year, as suggested by "Welcome Home!" signs at park entrances. In addition to busy activity schedules, large Yuma parks have stage shows and dances with live musicians.

Country Roads has been the most exclusive and expensive of the area RV resorts, although is now largely populated with park models. The new Palms RV Resort has an impressive website, advertising large greenbelt lots starting at $80,000 (in 2011) on which casitas can be built, and touting many features including a massage salon and dog grooming. Winter rentals at the Palms start at around $800 a month.

Once a busy river port, among Yuma's attractions are the **Yuma Territorial Prison** (once "the hellhole of Arizona"), the Yuma Crossing State Historic Park, Fort Yuma, river tours, golf courses, casinos, and the proximity to Mexican border towns. Lute's Pub and Casino (no gambling) in Old Town is a popular hamburger joint and according to *Trailer Life* "the oldest continuously active pool hall and domino parlour in the state".

Snowbirds stream to **Algodones,** Mexico (a few miles west and south) for cheap prescription drugs, dental work, eye glasses, and margaritas, most crossing the border on foot. "Sidewinder Days" in December and March show Algodones' appreciation for its winter clientele.

Yuma Lakes, the CRA park north of town, accepts only members in peak time. Further north still, right on the River, is Hidden Shores, more expensive than the Yuma parks and with limited activities, but with many waterview sites. To the west is the highly-rated Cocopah RV Resort with its own golf course and great doggie park.

Quartzsite

Usually a truck stop on I-10 twenty miles from the California border, in January and February more than a million RVers converge on the lands surrounding Quartzsite to inspect the gigantic desert bazaar which takes over the town, and to share the camaraderie of fellow snowbirds. The Big Q in winter has been described as "more a phenomenon than a place", where "shopping and haggling have been referred to as an art form". With its roots in the rock/gem business forty some-odd years ago, the annual **Rock and Gem Show** is still the main attraction.

The town itself has a number of basic RV parks with hook-ups (most of which are expensive and do not accept pets), but a large part of the fun is setting up camp in the surrounding desert lands with hundreds of thousands of fellow RVers. Something every RV snowbird should do at least once. The southeast quadrant of the I-10/I-95 junction appears to be the most desirable Quartzsite boondocking location.

Phoenix and the Valley of the Sun

With the advent of air conditioning **Phoenix** grew quickly into one the country's largest cities, with impressive educational, medical, shopping, and recreational facilities, as well as ballet, opera, symphonic music, Broadway plays, rock concerts, fashion shows, museums, art exhibits, and a wide choice of restaurants. It has also become one of the country's most popular retirement and snowbird destinations.

Theme parks and water features are obviously not important to the swarms of snowbirds who annually fill the dozens of walled and gated RV resorts in the satellite cities east of the capital. **Mesa** has the greatest concentration of snowbird megaresorts in America, all with good security, extensive amenities, busy winter activity programs, and usually over 1000 sites (Mesa Regal RV Resort has 2005). Most Phoenix-area parks charge around $600 a month, although the newer ones in the picturesque desert settings east of Apache Junction are more.

With only about 10% of their sites available for drop-ins, most Valley resorts are not ideal for itinerant snowbirds. Phoenix parks also have strict pet regulations, many disallowing them and the others segregating them. I-10 travelers can bypass the city completely by taking Highway 85 south at mile 112 to Gila Bend on I-8, and there is now a ring road south of Phoenix for those heading east.

The Central Corridor

Less than an hour south of the capital, **Casa Grande** has become a popular winter destination for RVers, with a number of snowbird parks (including a WHR location), factory outlet stores, and all necessary services. More short-term RV spots are available than in Phoenix and prices are generally lower although Palm Creek RV Resort, with a golf course, impressive facilities, and over 1500 sites, charges over $600 a month in prime time. Tom and Stephanie Gonser, from rversonline.org, speak highly of the local BeDillons restaurant.

Thirty miles further is the considerably cheaper Picacho Peak Resort, and to the east near Florence are several charming rustic parks and Desert Gardens which has recently undergone extensive upgrades.

Small desert park near Florence

The Deep South

Continuing down I-10 you finally come upon saguaro cactuses, the stereotypical symbol of the desert. This part of the state, with craggy mountains, the changing faces of the Sonoran Desert, and breathtaking sunsets, rivals the grandeur of its canyons to the north. Artists love the region and chances are you will too.

Located two hours south of Phoenix, **Tucson** is an historically rich city with strong Mexican and Native American roots and snow-topped mountains. In spite of its picturesque setting and clean air, lower temperatures (because of its altitude) deter many long-term winter visitors. Voyager, Rincon East, and Rincon West Resorts are comparable in size, activities, and price to Mesa's megaresorts, but, incorporating more greenery and desert plants into their landscaping, are more attractive than most of the Phoenix area parks. There are also a number of appealing smaller campgrounds in the surrounding desert lands. Tucson is definitely worth a visit, including a mandatory day at the **Arizona-Sonora Museum**, and possibly a trip to the Biosphere, Old Tucson Wild West Park, Saguaro National Park (to the west and to the east of the city), and time at the artisans' shops in Old Town.

Out and About

Many visitors to Tucson continue on an hour or so southeast to the **Kartchner Caverns**, the wild-west town of **Tombstone**, and the old mining village of **Bisbee**, in an interesting desert area with several membership parks, which being cooler and off the beaten track are likely to have vacancies.

In the northern part of the state, an area too cold for winter RV living, you will find views which have filled the pages of *Arizona Highways* magazines for over 70 years, and you can't visit Arizona without seeing the Grand Canyon (only the South Rim is open in the winter). There is a $25 vehicle fee to enter the National Park, or you can purchase an annual America the Beautiful pass, good in all National Parks, for $80 (in 2011). Also try to fit in trips to the Painted Desert, Petrified Forest, Salt River Canyon, and beautiful Sedona/ Oak Creek region.

Grand Canyon

As access to many of these locations in the winter will involve snow-covered roadways, it is best to leave the rig at the RV park and use discount coupons in one of the tourist booklets for low-priced accommodation. Even in good weather Highway 89A north of **Sedona** is too narrow and curvy for large RV's, but don't let that keep you away—in the tow vehicle.

According to the Arizona Office of Tourism close to half a million Canadians visit the state each year, probably most of them snowbirds. Check out arizonaguide.com or call 888 520-3448 or -3445 for further information on the Grand Canyon State.

Southern Texas—for Birding, Dancing, and Affordability

It doesn't have the scenery of Arizona or Southern California, or the theme parks of Florida, but south Texas does have snowbird-friendly weather, a Chamber of Commerce in the Rio Grande Valley claiming the area "really has only two seasons—summer and maybe I'll bring a jacket". The climate offers activities for all outdoor enthusiasts, and for birders, Mexico aficionados, history buffs, square dancers, and low-budget golfers, southern Texas is *the* place to be.

With snowbirds and retirees the backbone of the economy, and no major interstate highway charging through, the Tip of Texas has a more easy-going lifestyle than greater Palm Springs, Phoenix, or Orlando. There are fewer monster trucks, fewer sirens, and fewer cellphones at the wheel. South Padre Island has a local ordinance banning ties.

Unknown to many, Texas has beautiful **beaches**—South Padre's one of America's top ten. Although the water is too cold for swimming in the winter months, the coastal areas are popular year-round with fishermen, boaters, and beachcombers.

RV parks and fuel cost less than at the other snowbird destinations. Texas beef is also relatively cheap and the locally grown Ruby Red grapefruit are a real deal. With few high-end boutiques and no outlet malls, shopping expeditions are limited to Walmarts and Mexico. Peter Piper Pizza and Shoney's are 'bout as fancy as dinin' gits. (Actually Corpus Christi and South Padre Island offer more high-class establishments.)

Kenny Rogers performed in McAllen when we were there a few years back, but entertainment for Texas snowbirds is usually cards, billiards, jam sessions, and dances in the clubhouse. There are greyhound races in Harlingen and The Texas Treasure Casino 9 miles offshore from Port Aransas (as well as one in the middle of nowhere at Eagle Pass, between Del Rio and Laredo), but bingo or penny poker at the park are the only gaming alternatives. In Sunbelt Texas there is little to upset the budget.

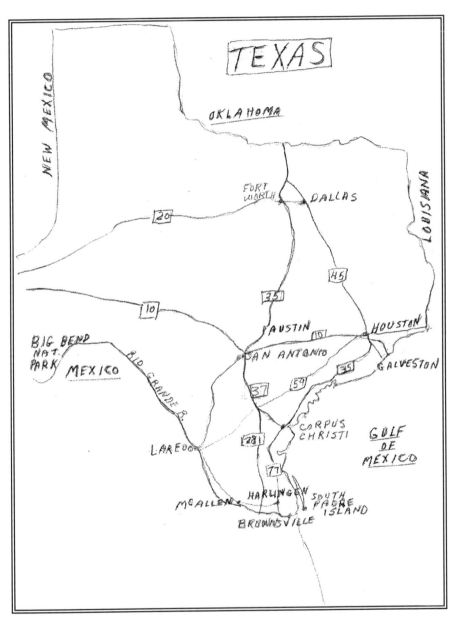

Map of Texas

In addition to impressive major thoroughfares, the state has thousands of farm roads, county roads, and spur roads, numbered in no apparent sequence. (Paul suggested they were named in the order they were built.) A map of the Rio Grande Valley is a must for visitors. The "Drive Friendly" signs along the Texas freeways are a nice touch, and free wi-fi at interstate rest stops and some state campgrounds commendable.

But beware of Texas-sized potholes–on side roads and in campgrounds and parking lots. One night we changed our dinner plans to McDonald's takeout in order to get home before dark when the ominous craters along our route could devour the Saturn. The holes are particularly hazardous when full of rainwater.

America's second largest state actively promotes its Deep South as a winter destination. Cities in the main snowbird locations–the Rio Grande Valley, South Padre Island, and the Coastal Bend around Corpus Christi–have special activities, discounts, welcome signs, and "Days" and "Weeks" for "Winter Texans". Quite different from another snowbird destination with the reported attitude: "If this is snowbird season, can we shoot them?"

Campgrounds

Of the hundreds of RV parks catering to Winter Texans, few are of the calibre of the major resorts in Southern California, Arizona, and Florida. There are no elite Outdoor Resorts and thus few Newells and Beavers. But rates are much less than comparable parks in the other snowbird states–typically around $350 a month.

As everywhere, facilities vary greatly from location to location, although virtually all parks have a pool, clubhouse, and winter social program of some type. Texas' largest park, Fun 'n Sun in San Benito with almost 1500 sites, claims to have "the most extensive activity program in the Texas Tropics"– including dances with the Fun 'n Sun Band, luaus, Mardi Gras celebrations; pool (10 tables) and shuffleboard (20 indoor courts) leagues; and social, line, square, round, tap, and clogging dance lessons, to name but a few of the possibilities. The park has its own TV channel to help you keep track. Winter rates in 2011 are around $600 a month plus electricity. (Almost all Texas RV parks have metered electricity.)

A large number of south Texas RV resorts are **retirement communities** with good recreational facilities and programs, but also many actual homes and park models, including Fun 'n Sun and the highly rated Victoria Palms in Donna. As mentioned before, most RVers prefer to be with other rigs, rather than nestled between permanent structures.

There are a Thousand Trails park and a Western Horizon location; several Coast to Coast, RPI, and AOR campgrounds; plus a number of non-**membership** affiliates and discount club offerings in the Texas Sunbelt. For real sun-lovers, "America's southern-most deluxe nudist RV resort" (Sandpipers) is located near Edinburg.

The Rio Grande Valley

The highest concentration of Winter Texans gathers north of the Rio Grande River, which forms the Mexico/U.S. border, mainly along the fifty mile strip between Mission and Harlingen. In addition to the multitude of RV parks in the so-called Rio Grande Valley (although there are no hills), the area boasts world class medical centers, a Camping World outlet, and seemingly dozens of Whataburger locations. It can be breezy.

The city of **McAllen** is the undisputed "Square Dance Capital of the World", with over 10,000 dancers arriving each winter. "The World's Largest Beginners' Square Dance Class" is held weekly in January, and a Texas Square Dance Jamboree later in the season. The "City of Palms" (one of many in the U.S) also hosts an annual Winter Texan Expo and Winter Texan Talent Show. The Chamber of Commerce claims that "two-thirds of the Valley's 500 plus RV parks are located in the McAllen area, with over 40,000 spaces available".

Harlingen is considered the most sophisticated city in the Valley as well as "the antique capital". Its revitalized Jackson Street District features architecture from the 1920's to 50's, and murals on over 30 buildings depict the history and flora and fauna of the area. The city is also home to the Valley Greyhound Park, with entertainment and dining in addition to races.

Brownsville, 20 miles to the south, is noted for its Mexican-American and Civil War battle sites, the Gladys Porter Zoo which specializes in endangered species, and Charro Days, a four-day Mardi Gras the end of February. The city is the south-ernmost population center in the mainland United States and a major entry to Mexico.

The Valley has a strong **Hispanic** flavour—seen in the abun-dance of Spanish radio and television channels, signs, and people (many of whom speak Spanglish). Tourists frequently cross the River into Reynosa, Matamoros, or Nuevo Progreso for shop-ping, sightseeing, dining, or entertainment, most parking on the American side to avoid buying Mexican automobile insurance. American money is readily accepted in the border towns.

On a natural flyway between North and South America, the Rio Grande Valley is one of the country's top **birding** destinations, with around 600 varieties documented. There are numerous sanctuaries, refuges, parks, and nature centers, many of which offer programs and tours. The 2008-acre Santa Ana National Wildlife Refuge near Alamo, claims the national record for bird sightings in one day and offers a tram tour in the winter months. Birders should consider camping at Bentsen-Rio Grande State Park, home of the World Birding Center Headquarters.

With the largest number of **butterfly** species in the U.S., the North American Butterfly Association has a 100-acre park near Mission, for education, conservation, and scientific study. There is also a large butterfly garden in Weslaco's Valley Nature Center. Information and brochures on bird and butterfly sites can be ob-tained from tourist information outlets.

It has been claimed that there are "probably more **golf** days in the Rio Grande Valley than just about any place else in the na-tion". Courses are less numerous and less impressive than most in Florida, Arizona, and greater Palm Springs, but they are also much less expensive. The Shary Municipal Course in Mission is an especially good value, and south Texas' best is purported to be the South Padre Island Golf Club, home of the Texas Senior Open.

I assume the turf on the links is different from the scrubby grass in south Texas campgrounds–a coarse variety with "sand spurs", which adhere to clothing and pet fur and burrow into bare feet and doggie paws. Experienced Texas campers set out carpet runners around their rigs and often out to the roadway.

Mission, at the western end of the main Valley strip, offers a selection of particularly inexpensive RV parks, and ninety miles further still is **Zapata**, where Sunset Villa, a nice Mom and Pop operation on Lake Falcon, "the best bass fishing lake anywhere", in 2011 still charges $100 to $120 a month (the same as in 2004). Many of the Rio Grande parks are operated by Wilder, Follett Resorts, Sunburst, or Encore, the latter two the same company.

The Winter Texan Times keeps visitors informed on wa's happnin' in the Valley–mainly sales, dances, and entertainment at the various RV parks.

South Padre Island

Beach lovers and anglers will prefer South Padre Island, a 34-mile long, half-mile wide barrier reef, which is often included as part of the Rio Grande Valley. The Island's high-rise hotels and condominiums present a striking skyline on its only approach over the two-mile Queen Isabella Causeway, the longest bridge in Texas.

The Island takes tourism very seriously, in snowbird season hosting a Winter Texan Golf Classic, Winter Texan 8 Ball Tournament, Winter Texan Fishing Seminar, Chili Cook-Off and Tradeshow, Rotary Winter Texan Fish Fry, and an annual Winter Texan Appreciation Week. Club Padre encourages interaction between island residents and visitors through social, recreational, cultural, and education programs.

Cutting through the long grasses and wetlands near the brilliant yellow Convention Center with its #53 Wyland Whaling Wall, is the 1500 foot Laguna Madre Nature Trail, a boardwalk constructed of recycled materials, for secluded viewing of birds and other wildlife, including alligators. **Nature lovers** should also visit the Laguna Atascosa Wildlife Refuge across the bay. Most of the island is undeveloped and Padre Island National Seashore on North Padre Island is reached on road only by way of Corpus Christi.

Winter Texan 8 Ball Championship
Open 2004

Paul Spink
Lazy Palms Ranch

Highlight of Paul's time on South Padre

The Gulf of Mexico and Laguna Madre (between the island and the mainland) have excellent **fishing** including flounder, trout, redfish, kingfish, wahoo, tuna, marlin, whiting, drum and sailfish, with charters available from Port Isabel across the causeway. Dolphin-watching tours, all types of boating, windsurfing, wind-kiting, and parasailing are also popular. Waverunners, hobie cats, jet skis and wet suits can be rented.

Isla Blanca County Park, with close to 600 full hook-up sites, a beautiful beach and impressive paved walking/biking trail, is among the best camping values in south Texas ($320 to $396 a month in 2011). Many of the more desirable sites are reserved a year in advance, although the only waterfront locations are in the overflow parking area, used only when all other spots are taken.

If you don't stay on South Padre, at least consider a day with a picnic lunch at Isla Blanca (small vehicle entrance fee), enjoying the beach and winter surf, and perhaps visiting the University of Texas Pan American Coastal Studies Lab with displays of fish and other marine life indigenous to the region.

Andy Bowie County Park, with some basic hook-up sites and a dry camping area, is across the highway from the Convention Center and a short walk over the sand dunes from the beach. The waterfront South Padre KOA, with more amenities and activities, charges considerably more than the county parks.

With Sheraton and Radisson Hotels and numerous restaurants, dining opportunities are more diverse than in the Valley. In 2004 we enjoyed a $9.95 all-you-can-eat seafood buffet at the Gulf Coast Oyster Bar.

Usually quiet, the Island gets wild during Spring Breaks in February and March, with the arrival of college students.

The Coastal Bend

Marshy lands and shallow bays have discouraged tourist development along most of Texas' Gulf coast, except around Corpus Christi and Rockport/Fulton, and on Mustang Island, all of which have good sandy beaches.

A city of about 300,000, **Corpus Christi**'s attractions include the Texas State Aquarium; the USS Lexington aircraft carrier and naval museum; the Museum of Science and History with life-size replicas of the Columbus ships, the Pinta and Santa Maria; and the Bayfront Arts and Science Park. Fishing, tennis, golf, windsurfing, and boating are popular in and around the "Sparkling City by the Sea". Much of nearby (North) Padre Island National Seashore, with nature trails and birding sites, is accessible only to hikers and four-wheel drive vehicles.

There are several RV parks in the city itself, but half an hour away on **Mustang Island** is the once funky fishing village of **Port Aransas** which, despite new beachfront highrise condos and hotels, still maintains some city- and county-operated camping on the beach. Check with the ranger and tide schedule before settling in on the on the sand.

Sites at the popular Pioneer Beach Resort, where the water is a few hundred yards over grass-covered dunes, in 2011 range from $440 a month for a standard back-in site to $700 for a pull-through. More expensive is Gulf Waters RV Resort, which has been described by Stephanie Gonser (of rversonline.org) as "a condo park of about 200 beautifully landscaped sites". More basic and less costly is On the Beach RV, and further south is a state park with beach camping (tide permitting) and some hook-up sites over the dunes.

Port A has much to offer visitors—a library where you can actually take out books, a computer resource center, numerous watering holes and restaurants, great fishing, the Texas Treasure gambling ship, golfing at Dune Crest, and three birding centers on the Great Coastal Birding Trail. In 2004 there was a fifty-cent bus trip to Corpus Christi and free trolley around town (and to the RV parks).

The **Rockport/Fulton** area to the north also has a variety of RV parks (including a Western Horizon location with resident alligators), and excellent fishing and birding. The Aransas National Wildlife Refuge 30 miles east, is the winter home to whooping cranes and good for 'gator viewing. Rockport's Texas Maritime Museum is also worth a look. The nearby Big Fisherman Restaurant is a popular dining spot.

Fishing near Rockport

The winter weather is not nearly as desirable on "The Texas Riviera" as in the Valley, with January highs and lows around 65 and 45 degrees and frequent rain and fog, but it is preferable to ice and snow.

Side Trips

In addition to requisite trips to Mexico, one should think about visiting **San Antonio** with the Riverwalk and Alamo, and **Houston** with the NASA Space Center and Astroworld. Consider taking advantage of low winter hotel rates advertised in the state's *Traveler Discount Guide,* saving fuel and avoiding the stress of city driving in the RV. There are now Caribbean cruises out of Galveston.

History enthusiasts will enjoy the old homes, churches, and cemeteries in cities such as Galveston; the abandoned forts of west Texas; the missions along the Rio Grande; and the numerous battle sites, particularly that of the first battle of the Mexican-American war near Brownsville and the battlefield of San Jacinto near Houston, where independence from Mexico was won. The state has about 1500 historical markers, many along Military Road (south of the Valley population centers), which is an interesting alternative route to the freeway.

Big Bend National Park, although hundreds of miles from the snowbird gathering spots, but not far off I-10, has spectacular scenery–canyons formed by the Rio Grande, volcanic peaks, and badlands.

Canada's snowbird migration (mainly RVers) to the Lone Star State is large enough for an annual rally of the Canadian Snowbird Association, usually held at the South Padre Island Convention Center. If you would like to become a Winter Texan check out traveltex.com or call 800 888-8TEX to order the state's impressive information package, which includes maps, the official state travel book, and an RV travel guide with a discount card for participating parks. Visitors should also consider purchasing a Texas State Park Pass for about $60, good for admittance to state parks, plus discounts for camping, state historic sites, and programs such as birding tours.

FLORIDA—FOR WATER, THEME PARKS, AND BIG OL' GATORS

Of all the snowbird states, Florida offers the most extensive directory of things to do. Whether you're a fisherman, boater, golfer, naturalist, shopper, casino buff, sports fan, jock, beach bum, or theme park junkie–Florida is for you. The weather can be humid, and there are frequent thunderstorms, but hurricanes are on hiatus during snowbird season.

It has been called the "World's Largest Water Park"–with 8500 miles of tidal shore that encompasses 8800 lakes, 320 springs, and 35 rivers. The coastal waters, only 60 miles from any point in the state, are too chilly for winter swimming except in southernmost locations, but the sandy shores welcome beachcombers, shell-collectors, hikers, picnickers, and sunbathers.

Boating is popular in the Gulf and Atlantic waters as well as the inland lakes, particularly with sports fishermen drawn by over 600 species. Anglers are also often seen **fishing** from Florida bridges, docks, and shorelines. Lake Okeechobee is one of several lakes in the United States claiming to have "the best bass fishing in the world". Canoeists and kayakers have many choices, including the calm waters of the intracoastal waterways. The coral reefs off the Atlantic coast and the clear rivers north of Tampa attract **snorkelers** and **scuba divers**.

The state has over 1100 **golf** courses (many with water views), more than 2000 miles of developed **hiking** trails (including the 1100 mile Florida Trail and Canaveral National Seashore), flat terrain for **biking** (notably on the 110 mile dike surrounding Lake Okeechobee and in the White Springs/Suwanee Valley area), and a multitude of man-made attractions (most around Orlando–Theme Park Capital of the World).

For **nature** lovers, in addition to the beaches and hiking trails, there are the Everglades, the Keys, and the Nature Coast south of Tallahassee, with hundreds of varieties of birds and water and land animals. Alligators seem to hang out in most every Florida water hole, but American crocodiles live only along the Everglades gulf

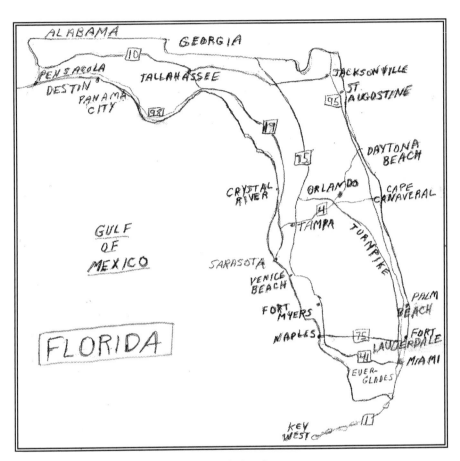

Map of Florida

coast. Miniature key deer (24"-30") inhabit Big Pine Key exclusively, manatees (sea cows) winter in the western rivers, and a small population of panthers roam the Everglades. All of the above, except alligators, are endangered.

For **sports** enthusiasts there are NFL, NBA, NHL, and big league baseball teams. Particularly popular with snowbirds are March baseball spring training camps and preseason games. There are also bigname golf and tennis tournaments, greyhound and swamp buggy races, and the Daytona 500.

The Fort Lauderdale Swap Shop and Circus, with more than 2000 vendors on 80 acres, is the state's largest flea market. A few miles to the west is America's biggest outlet mall–the alligator-shaped Sawgrass Mills, with 2.2 million square feet, more than 350 stores, over 20 movie screens, 11,000 parking stalls, and around 20 million customers annually. Miami has the high-end Bal Harbor Shops, Coconut Grove **shopping** district, and lively Bayside Marketplace.

Miami and Fort Lauderdale are also busy ports for a wide selection of low-priced Caribbean **cruises**.

Once an anti-gambling stronghold with gaming offered only offshore, the state now has widespread **casinos**, mainly in hotels. Sterling Cruise Lines still offers the best bang for your gaming buck, with a free five/six hour sail from Port Canaveral, including drinks while gambling, buffet, and Las Vegas style entertainment. Call 800 ROL-L711 for information and reservations.

With the highest percentage of **senior citizens** in the U.S., Florida caters to its elderly residents with senior days in retail outlets, discounted rates at entertainment venues, and early bird specials in restaurants. Shoney's gives free beverages to couples married over 50 years. Cracker Barrel has RV-sized parking stalls and endorses overnight parking.

Florida has an excellent highway system, although frequent congestion in the large population centers and a steady stream of vehicles on single-lane U.S. 1 in the Keys. A few dollars spent on toll roads (notably Florida's Turnpike) and bridges (in St. Petersburg) is worth the savings in time and fuel. The toll charge increases with the number of axles.

With 190 foot Mount Dora the highest mountain (outside the Panhandle), the flat straight thoroughfares are a dream for drivers of big rigs. Rest stops along the Florida interstates have 24 hour security, but do not permit overnighting. Consider purchasing Dave Hunter's *Along Florida's Expressways*.

Campgrounds

The first "tin can tourists" arrived in Florida from the North in the 1920's with Model T-towed trailers. Ninety years later the state has many hundreds of RV resorts, most catering to retirees and snowbirds with discounted long-term rates, activity programs, and sometimes age restrictions. A few have water-front locations (usually man-made lakes), some with paddle-boats and fishing piers. Others are hidden away in dark wooded areas, carpeted with dead leaves, and overrun with Spanish moss (which apparently is neither). Most have grass, a good number of trees, individual garbage pickup, and no electrical surcharge.

With the high cost of Florida real estate, **membership parks** are not cost effective, although there are two Thousand Trails properties; some Coast to Coast, RPI, and AOR affiliates; and numerous discount camping club locations. The "Encore" system (associated with Equity Lifestyles, which owns most Thousand Trails properties plus many others) appears to be the dominant player in the state. Walmart is not in the campground business in Florida, displaying "No Overnighting" signs at most of its stores.

The majority of Florida's privately-owned RV resorts sell or lease lots and are usually, at least in part, **retirement communities** with actual homes bunched throughout the park. (Again, not ideal for RVers.) Resorts in the southern third of the state are generally more attractive and offer more facilities and activities than those in the northern and central sections. They are also more expensive, costing from $700 to over $5000 a month (for a waterfront site at Bluewater Key), compared with $400 to $600 further north.

Florida also has an extensive system of **state campgrounds** with wilderness locations offering at least water and electricity, but limited amenities and pet restrictions. Bahia Honda, on one of America's top-rated beaches in the Keys, is among the most popular. State park sites can be reserved eleven months in advance at 800 326-3521.

Florida Camping by Marilyn Moore, Tom Dubocq, Sally Deneen, and Robert MacLure, gives an overview of the state's campgrounds.

South Florida RV resort

Miami and the Gold Coast

After being named one of the world's most dangerous tourist destinations in the early 1990's, increasing and retraining its police force and an aggressive public awareness campaign resulted in a restoration of Miami's tarnished image. Caution is still advised, particularly in poor neighbourhoods such as Liberty City, Overtown, Little Haiti, and Opa Locka.

With a strong link to Latin America (and the drug trade), Miami is a city of contrasts in ethnicity, opulence and poverty, beauty and urban blight. Visitors flock to **Miami Beach,** on a barrier island two miles from the mainland, whose South Beach is a playground for the rich and famous and a fascinating spot to study the art deco architecture and passing parade, plus visit the upscale boutiques, hotels, restaurants, and nightclubs. Nearby **Biscayne Key** attracts nature enthusiasts.

Many celebrities and affluent Americans have second (or third, or fourth) homes along the Gold Coast between Miami and Palm

Beach—including Donald Trump, with his Mar-a-Lago estate. The area is also a magnet for condo-staying snowbirds from eastern Canada, but the land is too high-priced for RV parks. Leave the rig at the campground and using your *Travelers' Discount Guide* for accommodation, take a side trip along scenic highway SRA1A between the Atlantic beaches and intracoastal waterway, with its magnificent homes and yachts. A humbling experience.

The Orlando Area, East and North

Since the opening of **Walt Disney World** in 1971, the Orlando/Kissimee/St. Cloud area has become the hub of Florida's tourist activity. On 28,000 acres, the Disney complex includes The Magic Kingdom, Epcot Center, Disney-MGM Studios, Disney's Animal Kingdom Theme Park, Discovery Island, Blizzard Beach, Typhoon Lagoon, golf courses, numerous resort hotels, a shopping and entertainment district, plus Fort Wilderness Resort and Campground.

Fort Wilderness, on 740 acres with 784 secluded sites surrounded by lush vegetation, offers many amenities and a boat ride to The Magic Kingdom. Check the Internet or call 800 WDISNEY for rates and availability. A large number of RVers choose one of the many lower-priced campgrounds in Kissimmee or St. Cloud, or visit the area by car and stay in a nearby hotel or motel.

Just down the road from Disney are Sea World of Florida, Universal Studios Florida, and Discovery Cove where you can swim with the dolphins. Discounts are often available for AAA members, except at the Disney parks, for which you should purchase a multiday/multipark pass from a travel agency at home. Disney World, Universal Studios, Sea World, and Fort Wilderness provide kennels. Orlando attractions should be avoided during school holidays and weekends.

Fifty miles to the east are the **Kennedy Space Center** and Cape Canaveral. Fifty-seven miles northeast is 23-mile-long **Daytona Beach**, home of the Daytona 500 in February, magnet for college students during Spring Breaks, and year-round draw for tourists, who often drive on the packed sand. **St. Augustine**, an hour further up the coast, is the oldest continuously occupied European settlement in the United States.

There are a large number of reasonably priced RV parks in central Florida, including numerous membership affiliates.

The Gulf Coast

More than a million acres have been reserved by the state for conservation and recreation 140 miles along the Gulf Coast north of Tampa, and U.S. Highway 19 has been officially designated the **Nature Coast Trail**. With world-renowned freshwater springs, vast forest preserves, and wetlands abundant with wildlife, the region is a paradise for naturalists. Of special interest are **manatees**, a species of playful sea cows ten to fifteen feet long and weighing up to 3000 pounds, who are particularly prevalent in the warm winter waters of the Crystal River. Pontoon boat rentals and glass-bottom and jungle boat trips are available.

The coast south of **Tampa Bay**—less expensive, less developed, less crime-ridden, and more relaxed than the Atlantic Gold Coast—is growing quickly as a tourist/snowbird destination, its gorgeous white sand beaches within easy driving distance from many snowbird parks in the southern part of the state. Busch Gardens (a 335 acre theme park incorporating one of the nation's largest zoos), the Florida Aquarium, the Museum of History and Industry, St. Pete's 2400' pier, and the Ringling Museum in nearby Sarasota are top attractions in the Tampa/St. Petersburg area.

Sarasota marks the beginning of the high rent district. Sun-N-Fun RV Resort (featured in a previous chapter), with 1519 sites and its own traffic light on the adjacent highway, is Florida's largest and most developed park. Royal Coachman Resort has been nominated "The Best RV Park in the Nation" and describes itself as "breathtakingly beautiful".

To the south are **Venice**, "The Shark Tooth Capital of the World"; Fort Myers, "The City of Palms", location of the winter homes of Henry Ford and Thomas Edison; and nearby Sanibel and Captiva Islands, which are famous for their seashells and 6000 acre J.N. Ding Darling Wildlife Refuge. The stretch between Venice and Fort Myers received the brunt of Hurricane Charlie in 2004, particularly Punta Gorda, where many mobile homes and trailers were demolished.

The **Fort Myers/Fort Myers Beach** area has many RV snowbird/retirement communities, as well as Red Coconut RV Resort, the only RV park right on the Gulf in mainland south Florida. Siesta Bay is the area's most highly rated park.

The southernmost city of **Naples,** with beachfront estates known as Millionaires' Row and the most golf courses per capita in the United States, is the "Palm Beach of the Gulf Coast". Of the numerous RV parks, centrally-located Rock Creek Resort and rustic Kountree Campinn are among the most reasonably priced. The crème de la crème is the Crystal Lake RV Resort, with lushly landscaped waterfront lots and marble pads and limited to Class A motorhomes. Unfortunately Club Naples can no longer be accessed for $10 a night through AOR or Sunbelt USA.

The Everglades

Encompassing 1,500,000 acres of subtropical wilderness, Everglades National Park is the second largest in the contiguous 48 states (after Yellowstone), the Western Hemisphere's largest mangrove ecosystem, and the only place on earth where alligators and crocodiles cohabit. With vast expanses of sawgrass flats dotted with cypress trees, the Everglades is actually a slow-moving freshwater river 50 miles wide and a few inches deep flowing from Lake Okeechobee, most of which becomes a swamp, with thousands of small islands (hammocks) in the summer rainy season.

Home to numerous species of birds, animals, and plants, the Everglades is a haven for birdwatchers and nature lovers, who use the extensive boardwalk system looking for bobcats, herons, bald eagles, pelicans, alligators, crocodiles, and manatees. Bicycles, canoes, kayaks, and information on self-guided tours

Big ol' gator

are available at the Flamingo Ranger Station, 38 miles southwest of the Main Gate near Florida City.

Tram and boat tours are available at dozens of locations, within and outside of the national park, most along Tamiami Trail (Highway 41) and at Everglades City. (Airboats are used when there is a risk of vegetation becoming tangled in the boat's motor.) For Everglades information check the Internet or call park headquarters at 305 242-7700.

Several reasonably priced government **campgrounds** are located along Tamiami Trail, notably one on a lake a couple of miles east of the Visitors' Center in Big Cypress Park, and one to the west with water, washrooms, and showers. On Chokoloskee Island, in a tropical setting a short distance south of Everglades City, is an Outdoor Resorts property not limited to Class A's.

The Keys

The Florida Keys, four hours south of Miami, is a series of low-lying coral islands joined by a 113-mile highway and 42 bridges,

Outdoor Resorts Chokoloskee Island

the most scenic stretch the less developed islands beyond Seven Mile Bridge. The Keys are renowned for **fishing**, particularly around Marathon and Islamadora, which have been called "The Sportsfishing Capitals of the World". Because of the surrounding reef there are few sandy beaches, but **snorkeling and scuba diving** are popular, especially at John Pennekamp State Park near Key Largo, the first undersea park in the continental U.S., and at Dry Tortugas National Park, 68 nautical miles west of Key West.

The Keys draw more than 1.5 million visitors annually (plus cruise ship passengers), most heading to **Key West,** at the southernmost tip of the United States–90 miles from Cuba–where attractions include Earnest Hemmingway's home, Harry Truman's home, key lime pie, and Jimmy Buffet's Margaritaville Bar. After relocation of the cruise ships, "Sunset at Mallory Square" is again visible. Get there early to enjoy a free show with mimes, torch jugglers, tightrope walkers, unicyclists, and interesting street people. Key West is inundated with college students during Spring Breaks.

Usually laid back, prices and activity soar in the Keys with the arrival of the snowbirds, most of whom settle in at the **RV parks** spotted all along the islands. Encore's Sunshine Key RV Resort is the largest park with 405 sites, and Bahia State Park is the best deal. Tenting is popular in the Keys with the younger generation and motorcyclists. I have heard the area north of Seven Mile Bridge sometimes has a bad smell from the mango trees.

All pricey, the waterfront spots at Sugarloaf Key KOA are considerably more expensive than the lakefront sites at the less fancy Sunburst RV Resort next door. Bluewater Key RV Resort at mile marker 15.6 offers a large palm-enshrouded spot on the Atlantic for around $170 a night, or you can buy your own lot (in 2011) from $425,000 to $969,000 (up considerably since we were there in 2004)! Jabour's RV Resort is right downtown in Key West but Boyd's RV Resort, an attractive waterfront park five miles from mile marker zero, is a much better choice for big rigs.

As parking of vehicles over 20' is forbidden on the city's narrow busy streets, plan to leave the rig at the RV park, at the Welcome Center (not easy access), Zachary Taylor State Park, or one of the free city-designated parking zones on the outskirts of town and take the tow car, city trolley, or taxi. Consider a city tour on the Old Town Trolley or Conch (pronounced "konk") Train or rent a bike and follow the open-air tram to get the narration.

You don't have to dine at Sloppy Joe's or Crabby Dick's in expensive Key West to experience the Keys' culinary delights. We greatly enjoyed the mahi mahi sandwiches at Mangrove Mama's on Sugarloaf Key and the Cracked Egg Café on Big Pine Key.

If Key West would be more appealing without the long slow drive and expensive RV sites, consider the 3½ hour **Key West Express** passenger ferry from Fort Myers or Marco Island (south of Naples), with rates around $120 for a return ticket.

The Panhandle

Although most snowbirds prefer the higher temperatures and more dependable sunshine of the southern half of the state (about 12 degrees Fahrenheit difference in the daytime and 15 at night),

Key West landmark

some choose the **Emerald Coast** of the Panhandle, which has some of the country's best beaches, with wonderful white sugar sand.

Oceanfront campgrounds such as Magnolia Beach Resort in **Panama City** and Camping on the Gulf in **Destin** run around $800 a month. The facilities and activity programs are not as extensive as at most resorts in southern Florida, but both aforementioned parks have clubhouses, heated pools, and nearby restaurants, shopping, and entertainment outlets.

Five minutes from "The Top-Rated Beach in the U.S.A." in **Santa Rosa**, is the reasonably-priced Gregory E. Morrow RV Park in Topsail Preserve State Park, with gorgeous landscaping, private sites, a winter activity program, indoor pool, tennis courts, shuffleboard, and horseshoes. Thirty miles inland is **De Funiak Springs**, with several well-priced RV parks on nearby lakes, including the popular membership affiliate Sunset King Resort.

Most parks in the Panhandle cater to RVers rather than full-time residents.

Yes, the Sunshine State has it all. Check it out further online at visitflorida.com or call 800 605-8228 for an information package.

MEXICO—FOR BUDGET, BEACHES, AND BAD ROADS

Mexico has a colourful history, rich culture, friendly people, magnificent scenery, and lots of winter sunshine. In spite of substandard roadways, violent drug wars, and an unsafe water supply, the country, particularly Baja California and the upper west coast of the mainland, is a popular destination for RVing snowbirds—sometimes as a side trip from California, Arizona, or Texas.

Sun-drenched beaches are Mexico's main attraction, the majority of its visitors flying in and ensconcing themselves in an Americanized all-inclusive oceanfront hotel for a week or two. What a shame to go to a foreign land without exploring its culture and countryside.

As an RVer you can experience all that Mexico has to offer from your own home base. You can take in the beauty of the deserts, mountains, and jungles. You can explore historical and archaeological sites. You can interact with the Mexican people, share their customs, visit their churches, and browse in their markets. And also enjoy the sun-drenched beaches.

Mexico's thousands of miles of coastline offers limitless opportunities for **fishing**, **boating**, **snorkeling**, **scuba diving**, **beachcombing**, **swimming**, **birdwatching**, and **whalewatching**. The country would be great for **hiking** if there weren't warnings to stay on the beaten path. *Into a Desert Place* by Graham Mackintosh may tempt you to throw caution to the wind. Many RVers do bring or rent all-terrain vehicles and head into wilderness areas. **Off-roading** is particularly popular in Baja.

There are no outlet malls and fashion boutiques are limited to the five-star hotels, but there are lots of open-air markets and quaint **shops** with grand assortments of handicrafts, where you must always bargain—starting at 50% off the quoted price and never settling for less than a 25% discount. Most small retailers do not take credit cards and some close from two to four for a siesta. Aggressive street pedlars can be annoying.

Golf courses are found only in the resort areas–in Baja, at Loreto and Los Cabos. Theme-park tourists and casino buffs will not be happy in Mexico.

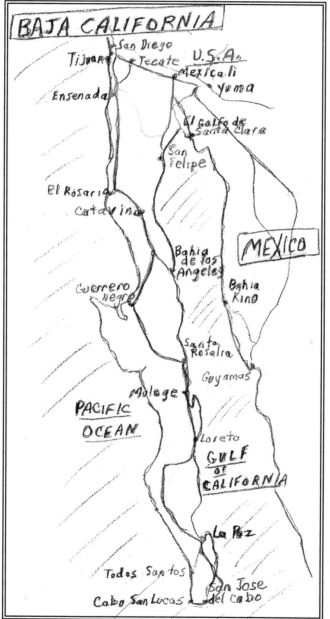

Map of Northwest Mexico

Topes, Tolls, and Potholes

Drivers of big RV's may also become disgruntled. Except for a few major highways linking large cities (which are mainly toll roads), most Mexican highways are narrow and two-laned with little signage and meagre or no shoulders, which prevents pulling over to allow passing. Sometimes a left turn signal means it is safe to pass, but it can also mean the driver is turning left!

Roads in Mexico are often poorly maintained–punctuated with potholes and sometimes littered with rocks, bottles, and dead animals. (*Freewheelin' USA* by Slater and Basch has a chapter entitled "Bouncing Down Baja".) In towns watch for *topes* (large speed bumps). Before heading out in the RV you may want to stuff a pillow or large towel in the dish cupboard, after putting coffee filters or paper towels between individual pieces.

Livestock, dogs, burros, and pedestrians often wander onto the roadways, and truck and long-distance bus drivers are fearless. One should drive defensively, ready to brake at any time and on occasion stopping for oncoming traffic. Drivers of wide-bodied rigs must be especially cautious, particularly on the curvas *pelugrosas* on mountain roads, where often there are no guard rails.

Mexican highway

Avoid travel at night, when cars and bicycles with no or faulty lights, sleeping animals, and an increased number of kamikaze truck drivers can be added to the aforementioned hazards. A breakdown in the dark can put you in a perilous situation—from other drivers rather than banditos, of whom everyone has heard, but few have seen.

As RV repair facilities in Mexico are limited, it is imperative your rig (particularly tires, brakes, and batteries) is in top condition when you enter the country. Many RVers take extra belts and hoses. On the plus side, a free government-operated road service called the **Green Angels** patrols the main highways carrying gas, oil, water, spare parts, and usually an attendant who speaks English. The Angels can be accessed by CB radio or toll-free at 800 903-9200, but they go off duty at 8 pm. A tip is customary.

The country has many **toll roads**, the price varying according to the number of axles on your vehicle combination, but there is almost always a free alternative. Sometimes it is an advantage to pay the toll, but often the free route is just as good. *The Traveler's Guide to Mexican Camping* by Mike and Terri Church analyzes the two options for each tollway, and makes the generalization: "Follow the trucks".

Expect **military checkpoints**, manned by baby-faced rifle-toting soldiers, on the lookout for guns and drugs. Often the "inspectors" will take the opportunity to practice their English. Keep an eye on valuables during the check.

The Baja AAA map indicates locations for gas and diesel, which are often few and far between. In wilderness areas you should fill up at every opportunity. There is no need for comparison shopping as all Mexican **fuel outlets** are operated by Pemex and have standard prices, as well as a cash-only policy. Diesel is available at three out of four stations, although its high sulphur content has been criticized. Propane can be bought in and near large population centers. Pemex stations encourage RVers to "pasar la noche" in their large patrolled lots. Check before settling in and give a small tip.

In Mexico your fuel tank often holds more than the capacity stated in the owner's manual. It is advised you specify the number of pesos rather than the quantity you want and observe the filling procedure. When buying oil watch that you are getting a full can. Again a small tip is appropriate.

Many RVers venturing into Mexico for the first time feel more secure traveling with at least one other party. **Caravans** (liberally advertised in RV publications) typically consist of a dozen or so rigs with a knowledgeable wagonmaster and a tailgunner, who is usually an experienced mechanic. In addition to leading the way to prechosen campgrounds, the wagonmaster buffets approaching trucks and gets you on the right road, which can be a challenge at the border. Many RVers dislike the regimentation, however, feeling that they can experience the country better on their own, at their own pace. A two-week Mexican caravan trek starts at about $800 per rig.

On most Mexican highways expect to travel an average of 35 to 40 miles per hour. Psych yourself out to drive slowly and cautiously and then enjoy the country.

Bribes and Banditos

In spite of anti-gun laws, in recent years there have been numerous well-publicized transgressions against tourists in Mexico, in addition to the murderous drug wars in border communities. Experienced travelers Mike and Terri Church claim that crime is no worse than in the U.S. and that they have never had trouble. Most echo their view.

As the majority of offences are due to Mexico's poverty, tourists should not reveal large amounts of cash, use a bank machine at night, or leave valuables in their vehicle. They should leave the Rolex at home, use a steel-reinforced money-belt, and avoid isolated areas, especially deserted beaches, even as a couple. It is also recommended one use only **taxis** dispatched by a respected hotel or called by a concierge rather than hailing one from the street, plus negotiate the fare ahead of time and write it down.

Mexico's crime problem is made worse by an ineffective justice system. Poorly paid **police** often do not follow up on reported crimes and sometimes look upon tourists as an opportunity to make a few pesos. They have been known to remove money while checking a wallet and to invent traffic infractions and issue a fine which is payable on the spot. If the driver hesitates or objects, often the amount will be lowered. The AAA guidebook recommends if you are unjustly accused: "Take the officer's [badge] number and ask to speak to his *jefe* (boss), or to be taken to the nearest *delegacion de policia*." Do not lose your temper as it is a serious offence to insult a police officer.

Veteran travelers to Mexico often just pay the fine, in which case the officer pockets the money, without writing up a citation–a practice known as ***mordida*** (bribery). The Mexican government is taking steps to curb police corruption, but in the meantime the best way to avoid such problems is to obey traffic rules scrupulously. (*ALTO* means *STOP!*) On the positive side, a few pesos can often buy you the right to double park, someone to watch over your vehicle, and a speedy border crossing.

Eat, Drink, but be Careful

Never drink, give your pet, or brush your teeth or wash contact lenses with, non-purified Mexican **water**, as the country's supply is contaminated by septic tanks and cesspools feeding sewage into the water table. Mexicans build up a tolerance, but the bacteria often attack northern immune systems, resulting in an intestinal upset which can last several days. Inexpensive 19-litre containers of purified water are available at supermarkets or from vendors who visit campgrounds. Use a hydro-pump (available at Camping World) rather than struggling with pouring.

For washing dishes and produce most RVers use boiled water with a few drops of bleach or chemical disinfecting tablets sold at pharmacies. For bathing some have a purification system installed in the rig, but most simply add about ¼ cup of bleach per 30 gallons of regular water in the freshwater tank and rely on a filtering system to remove the smell of chlorine.

Do not eat unpasteurized dairy products, food from street vendors, or anything which has not been cooked, boiled, or peeled by you–except in good restaurants, where you should still avoid sal-

ads and drinks with ice (although bagged ice is supposedly purified). Consider taking anti-diarrheal medications ahead of time, or
if your social calendar permits, eating a clove of garlic every day for
a week (there are less-aromatic alternatives available in the phar-
macy). Pepto Bismol, Immodium, or Lomatil, taken with tea and/
or juices, usually work against *turista*, but if you still feel dreadful
after 48 hours consult Mexico's well-reputed medical system. Many
get hepatitis shots before visiting the country.

Most foodstuffs are readily available, and your **grocery** bill
should be lower than at home. Fresh produce, tortillas, and beer
are particularly inexpensive. Also prawns—relatively speaking.
Fruit and vegetables are cheaper in public markets and you can
dicker on the price. It is advisable to bring your own cheese, butter,
peanut butter, pickles, and canned tomatoes—bearing in mind that
you are officially allowed to import only $50 per person in groceri-
es. (I have not heard of anyone being checked.)

Food and water should be carefully stored to discourage ants,
but as a precaution, ant traps, as well as insect repellent, should be
brought from home.

U.S. dollars are accepted in Baja and Mexican border towns, but
your money will go further if you change it into pesos before entering the country or at bank machines. (In mid-2011 the rate is approximately 12 pesos per Canadian dollar.) Most restaurants and
stores in tourist areas, as well as the larger supermarket chains and
Walmart take credit cards, but you will need cash for many smaller
shops and eateries, most campgrounds, and all Pemex stations.
ATM machines are not as widespread as in North America.

No Habla Espanol

Tourists usually manage just fine with English and sign language, but many take advantage of the opportunity to practice a
little Spanish. The AAA Mexico Tour Book has seven pages of
key vocabulary and phrases and of course there are more extensive guides. English-language newspapers and editions of *Time* and
Newsweek can be found in most large tourist centers. Shaw Direct
and DirecTV are the best systems for English television access.

Prepaid **Ladatel** phone cards, available at pharmacies and Pemex mini-marts, are the most economical way to handle outgoing calls, although not all pay phones accept them. Alternatively, you can get a special access number from your home phone company, which routes your calls through them rather than the expensive Mexican operator. Stay away from the "blue telephones", which accept credit cards but charge up to $30 a minute!

Do not expect **Internet** access at Mexican campgrounds. Track down an Internet Café and use their computers rather than your own. Standard cellphones will not work, but a chip replacement will provide local reception.

Campgrounds

Campgrounds in Mexico are generally far inferior to those in Canada and the United States. Most large ones in tourist areas have hook-ups, but the water will have to be treated, the sewer outlet will probably require an extra length of hose, and the electrical outlet will likely accommodate only two prongs, need an adaptor, and should be pre-tested for voltage and electrical faults. Few Mexican campgrounds are wired for power-hungry RV's with air conditioners and there will likely be frequent voltage drops. (Use a surge protector.) Three or four 120 volt table fans are recommended for keeping cool, as well as for keeping mosquitoes at bay.

Only 26 campgrounds in the entire country met the standards to be included in a recent AAA Mexico Travel Book, with half in Baja and only three receiving AAA's top rating. With increased demand, quality is improving, however, and KOA's are moving in. Many Mexican RV parks operate in conjunction with a large hotel, which allows use of its facilities.

Most campground **washrooms** have flush toilets, but you must provide your own soap and toilet paper, which in many places is to be deposited into a basket after use, as the plumbing system cannot handle it. There is generally at least one shower (sometimes in the adjacent hotel), but often no hot water. Predictably, washroom facilities are often unsanitary.

In most cases you will have to take laundry to town. You may want to pack a clothesline and pegs or portable drying apparatus for mini-washes.

Expect possibly cable, but no wi-fi, few recreation facilities, and no activity programs at Mexican campgrounds, but there will always be a fellow RVer ready to share experiences, and sometimes food and drinks.

Sand access roads and parking on the beach can cause problems for big rigs, notably at Golfo de Santa Clara, which is set up entirely on sand. A shovel, rake, boards, and a jack are recommended accessories for beach camping. Deflating tires will often help in a sand trap (if you have the means to re-inflate them). Beachfront sites in established RV resorts will be taken by permanent or seasonal residents, blocking the view and the breeze. Many beautiful waterfront locations remain vacant because of warnings against isolated camping.

The Church's *Traveler's Guide to Mexican Camping* reviews over 200 campgrounds, as well the major roadways, and dispenses other valuable information and advice. Don't leave home without it. They also now have a book specifically on Baja. Also recommended are Walt Peterson's *Exploring Baja,* Kathy Olivas' *Mexico by RV,* and David Eidell's mini-series on Mexico on the rversonline. org website.

Campground prices average around $20 a night. Reservations are difficult unless you speak Spanish, but are usually unnecessary, unless a caravan takes over a park.

La Garita International

To cross into Mexico you need proof of citizenship, a driver's license not adequate. If you are traveling further than 80 miles into the country (beyond Ensenada or San Felipe), or are staying longer than 72 hours, you also require a tourist card, which can be obtained at Mexican consulates in the U.S. or Canada and immigration offices at points of entry, for about $20.

For day trips visitors usually park on the U.S. side and walk into the country.

To drive in Mexico you must have special vehicle **insurance** and title and registration papers for all vehicles. The insurance can be purchased from private outlets, AAA offices near the border, or insurance companies advertising in RV publications. Shop around, as rates (all expensive) vary greatly. If you are going for over a month, it is often cheaper to take the annual rate. Most RVers planning to roost in one spot for a long period insure their tow vehicle for the entire Mexican stay, and the rig for only the time it will be on the highway, but consider that vandalism and storm damage will then not be covered on the RV. Check with your Canadian insurance company regarding a rebate for a lengthy stay in the country.

To curb illegal importation, vehicles traveling outside Baja must also have a temporary **vehicle permit**, which requires a major credit card as bond and proof of ownership. If there is a lien on the vehicle or if it is on loan or rented, you also need a notarized letter from the lender or owner giving permission to take the vehicle into the country. Again, permits are available at Mexican consulates and border immigration offices.

It is written that **pets** must have a health certificate from a veterinarian, issued not more than 72 hours prior to entry to Mexico, and proof of up-to-date immunizations, but customs officials never even glanced at Simba. Best not to fall in love with one of the many undernourished stray dogs in the country.

Many visitors get dental work and purchase cheap eyeglasses and prescription drugs in Mexico. In 2005 the allowance was 90 days of medication crossing back into California and 30 days worth into Arizona and Texas, purchased for personal use with a prescription in your name. Certain produce and meat items (including fresh chicken) are not allowed back into the U.S. An official list seems to be unavailable. We have simply been asked if we had fruit. Liquor allowances are the same as for Canada.

Baja California

Except for San Felipe in the northeast corner, all the major snowbird locations in Baja are in the southern half of the peninsula. From Tijuana to **Ensenada** the divided toll highway Mex I-D is like a continuation of I-5, and is safer, faster, and more scenic than Mex 1. The RV park at the Hotel Estero, 6 miles south of Ensenada, is a good place to spend the first night. From there on you have the *real* Mexican-type highway, with hundreds of miles of changing desert and rugged terrain, but few stretches with water views. Gas up at **el Rosario** for the long trip to **Guerro Negro** (known for its whale-watching). Check out the murals painted by the Cochmi Indians on the cave and canyon walls of the central desert region.

The stretch between Ensenada and **Catavino** (which is considered a dangerous town) is the worst part of the Transpeninsular Highway, but the once-atrocious secondary road to popular **Bahia de los Angelos** has been paved. The second half of the main highway is two feet wider and less mountainous than the northern section.

About halfway down is the town of **Mulege,** described as "an oasis in the middle of the inhospitable Baja California desert", and 12 miles south will be a large concentration of snowbirds camped on the beaches of **Bahia Concepcion**–many for the winter. Mulege offers restaurants, grocery stores, a Pemex station, Internet cafe, and finally banking facilities. There are no hook-ups on the beach, but fellow campers and locals can advise what to do about water and dumping. **Loreto** has an 18-hole championship golf course.

From Santa Rosalia or La Paz you can take a **ferry** to mainland Mexico–an interesting experience, particularly backing your RV off the vessel. Call toll-free 91-800-6-96-96 for reservations, as tickets cannot be purchased at the terminal. **La Paz** is a good-size city with lots of stores and campgrounds.

Finally, 1060 miles from Tijuana, you come to Cabo San Lucas and San Jose del Cabo (together referred to as **Los Cabos**), which to many are a disappointment after the scenery to the north. The area does offer a four-lane highway, lots of restaurants, tourist establishments, golf courses, and to the east a number of campgrounds. Most of the golf links are championship calibre averaging $200 a round, but Villan de Cortez, a 9-hole par 3, an hour to the north, in 2009 was only $20. Consider a visit to the art colony at nearby **Todos Santos.**

Land's End, Cabo San Lucas

Walt Peterson's *Exploring Baja* provides a mile by mile description of the Transpeninsular Highway, locations of Pemex stations, and information on attractions. The round trip can be made comfortably in 14 to 17 days.

The **border** crossing at Tecate is faster and easier than Tijuana for re-entry into the States. In Mexicali follow the signs for "*Garita Internationale*".

Mainland Mexico

For mainland Mexico, the easiest route is down the west coast on Mex. 15, a reasonably-priced four-lane toll road from Nogales, south of Tucson.

There is a CRA park at **Golfo de Santa Clara** at the mouth of the Colorado River (watch the sand) and a WHR/Sunbelt USA park at **Bahia Kino.** Some RVers take day treks to Kino Bay or **Guyamas**, but many continue on three days to **Mazatlan**, where rates are about $350 a month.

Although many of the prime campground locations have been taken over by condo developments, there are still oceanfront RV parks with hook-ups. The stretch between **San Blas and Puerto Vallarta** is a popular camping area, but the two-lane road south of Mazatlan is not as good as that to the north.

Consider staying on the outskirts of cities and using public transportation– for the savings and the experience. Also think about the railway trip to the **Copper Canyon** from **Los Mochis.** The Church's guidebook outlines trips to the **Yucatan Peninsula** on the east coast, the center of Mayan civilization, as well as other Mexican RV treks for the adventurous.

To encourage tourism, Mexico's #1 industry, road improvements and an overhaul of the police department are underway, and campgrounds, gas stations, and supermarkets are being built. Some towns such as San Felipe and Algodones have Snowbird Festivals in recognition of winter visitors.

A few, like the man I listened to sound off about Mexican roads in the Catalina Spa laundry, say, "Never again!", but most RV snowbirds (many Canadians) can't wait to return to their favourite spot in the Mexican sun each winter.

So it seems it has always been. Earl Stanley Gardner (creator of Perry Mason) wrote in the early sixties: "It is impossible to account for the charm of this country or its fascination, but those who are familiar with the land [*Baja California in this case*] are either afraid of it or they love it, and if they love it, they are brought back by irresistible fascination time and time again."

New Zealand–for Trekking, Sheep, and Driving on the Left

With its rugged mountains, tumbling waterfalls, rushing rivers, soaring geysers, spectacular coastlines, and glaciers abutting tropical forests, New Zealand has been described by James Michener as "probably the most beautiful country on the face of the earth", and by Rudyard Kipling as, "the eighth wonder of the world". Add exotic birds, marine mammals, and a rich Maori heritage to the scenic delights, and you have what *Lonely Planet* calls "a microcosm of the world's attractions". It is the ultimate snowbird destination.

The country is at its best during its summer season from November to March, when the weather forecast is almost always "fine" (an official meteorological term in New Zealand), with temperatures between 20 and 25 degrees Celsius. The North Island is hotter and the west coasts are wetter. From mid-December to the end of February the locals will also be enjoying the hiking tracks, sand, and water, but you will never feel like you are on Waikiki Beach.

New Zealand is a Shangri-La for **hikers** and **nature lovers**. The country's well-signed and -maintained trails vary in length from an hour to several days, multi-day walks providing (over 900) huts for sleeping and shelter. No predatory animals such as snakes, bears or foxes will be lurking in the lush vegetation.

Kiwi weather forecast

Maps and information on the "bush walks" are available at tourist centers.

Birders will be interested in the many species not found in North America, including albatross, kiwis, penguins, and the nearly extinct kakopo, takahe, taiko, kea, and kaki (black stilt). The country has several wildlife reserves and aviaries in addition to its abundance of marine mammals near Kaikoura and Dunedin.

With miles of indented coastline and mountain lakes, New Zealand is an idyllic place for **sailing, kayaking, canoeing, and fishing**. To the disdain of many, almost anywhere there is a navigable river you will also find high-speed jet boats. For the really adventurous there are mountain-climbing, whitewater rafting, river surfing, bungee jumping, skydiving, and canyon swinging–mainly in and around Queenstown.

Map of New Zealand

The country's 400+ **golf** courses range from world-class to those without sprinkler systems, which become brown in hot weather and where hitting a sheep gets you another shot. New Zealand's three-dimensional **mazes** were popular long before corn mazes in America, the best known at Puzzling World near Wanaka. There are **casinos** in Auckland, Queenstown, and Christchurch.

Shoppers will enjoy the shops and markets in Auckland, Christchurch, and Nelson, and the Maori handicrafts in the Rotorua area. Jade, sheepskin, and woolen goods are especially good value. ATM machines are abundant and major credit cards widely accepted. Retail and restaurant prices seem expensive, but the sticker price includes the goods and services tax. In mid-2011 one Canadian dollar is worth about 1.3 New Zealand dollars.

Even with direct **flights** from Vancouver, some still break up the long trip with stopovers in Hawaii or Fiji. (The Big Island of Hawaii has motorhome rentals.) Your passport must be valid for at least six months beyond your departure date and for a stay over three months you need an extended visitor's visa. The country demands a good guidebook and at least four weeks. Eight would be twice as good.

Campervans

Traveling by "campervan" is a popular way to explore the New Zealand countryside economically at your own pace. In addition to commercial campgrounds there is an excellent network of campsites in national parks, beach resorts, and urban areas, managed by the Department of Conservation.

Companies such as **Maui Motorhomes, Britz, United,** and **Kea** provide campground guides and maps with their rentals, which vary from about $50NZ to $200NZ daily, depending on the model, season, and length of rental. Check out kiwistyletravel.com for comprehensive coverage. A discount is usually available if you book well in advance, and if you pick up the RV in Christchurch on the South Island (where most are dropped off) you may be entitled to free airfare from Auckland or an interisland ferry crossing.

Campervan rentals are equipped with bedding, dishes, pots and pans, broom and dustpan, bucket (for draining the grey water), and clothespins(!). We wished there was also a door mat, dish rack, soap dish, and (with early darkness) a flashlight. The tiny bathroom is functional but we usually used the campground facilities. (FYI–your hair dryer will not work in New Zealand unless you have an electrical converter and 3-prong adapter, but many campground washrooms have dryers.)

For a visit of two months or more you may want to consider **buying** a van on arrival in Auckland or Christchurch and reselling on departure, using newspaper advertisements, *The Auto Trader*, or a dealership which will take the unit back when your travels are over. If buying privately look for a unit with a recent WOF (warrant of fitness) certificate and use the AAA inspection service. Also check out ownership, liens, etc. In a case described in the *RV Times*, a campervan purchased for $12,600NZ sold for $11,900 after five months and over 8000 kms.

Our campervan at a holiday park

RV owners from America have also had success with RV **swapping** in response to ads in RV publications and by using the homeholidayswap.com website.

The New Zealand Automobile Association has maps and tour books, as well as Top 10 and Kiwi Holiday Parks information, where reservations are advised November to April. A low-priced membership in the NZAA also gives 10% discounts at select parks, restaurants and attractions.

Holiday Parks

The country's "holiday parks" consist of cabins (and sometimes motels); tent and **power camping sites**; laundromats with outside drying carousels (reason for the clothespins); recreation rooms with TV's, games, and Internet stations; washrooms, including bathtubs for children and sometimes hairdryers; plus communal kitchens with stainless steel counters, sinks, fridges, ranges, and microwaves. Some have tennis courts, swimming pools, spa pools, and jumping pillows(!).

Occasionally power sites also have fresh **water** taps, but never **sewer** hook-ups. There are dump stations as in America, but we decided it was easier to do like the locals and dispose of grey water with the provided bucket and empty the cassette toilet by removing it rather than using the hoses. Using camp toilets and showers keeps waste water to a minimum. **Rates** for a power site are about the same as in North America, with card-carrying KOA members given a discount at Top 10 Parks.

Public telephones are in short supply in the country. At the award-winning Top 10 campground in Te Anau the only phone for guests was in a booth on the highway and the Visitors' Center in Wanaka had no public phone. Seek out an Internet site.

We always felt safe in New Zealand's holiday parks, rarely locking our doors in the daytime, and sometimes forgetting at night. (Not recommended.)

Along the Way

In addition to its breathtaking scenery, New Zealand is known for its friendly people (often called Kiwis) and numerous sheep–about 17 million of the latter to each of the former. Heavily dependent on agriculture and horticulture, the country has been referred to as "the world's biggest farm". (The green of its pasturelands and meadows rivals that of the Emerald Isle.) Visitors should take in one of the country's "farm shows" (starring sheep) and perhaps sample some of the country's 100 plus wineries.

Except near and within cities, New Zealand's **roads** are two-laned, with speed limits generally 100 kph. They are well-maintained, with good signage, frequent rest areas, and few big trucks, but many routes are narrow and winding, with one-way bridges. Beware of *jetter bars* (speed bumps) in some towns.

You soon get used to **driving** on the lefthand side, although for the first few miles expect to turn on the windshield wipers when you signal for a turn. On the highway it is no problem and in cities they have installed little blue signs at intersections to keep tourists on the right (actually, the left) track. Don't be intimidated by the traffic circles at major intersections–they work beautifully. In 2002 when diesel was almost half the price of gas, we were very pleased with our Maui Spirit 4 with the diesel-powered Mercedes engine.

"Tea Rooms" and "Takeaways" pop up every so often along major thoroughfares and of course there are McDonald's and Starbucks in the cities. Some **restaurants** allow you to bring your own wine and tipping is not expected (but becoming more common). Although our dining experiences were limited, I felt the country was not noted for its culinary delights. We enjoyed a number of good buffets, but lamb was expensive, and out of the six Kiwi pizzas we tried, Pizza Hut was by far the best. Paul was impressed with the price of Heineken beer.

You know **grocery shopping** will be an interesting experience when you are asked to "Obtain Trundler Prior to Entry". We could find no wieners, baloney, 2% milk, orange cheese, or doughnuts, but there were lots of capsicums (peppers), parsnips, cheap Gala apples, and many brands of muesli cereals and bars. Plan to visit a Pak 'n

Save outlet for your first big order. Remember to drive your trundler on the left side of the aisle.

It is recommended you bring coffee and reading material from home, and that you use a prepaid phone card or e-mail (perhaps Skype) rather than a calling card.

Be prepared for a rivalry between New Zealand and Australia, which Kiwis refer to as "the island to the north". An Australian once listed its adversary for sale on E-bay!

The North Island

International flights usually land in **Auckland,** a modern harbour city built on volcanic rock and home to about one third of the nation's population. As driving on the left side of the road for the first time with jet lag would not be fun, new arrivals should consider staying at the Manukau Top Ten Holiday Park, a few miles from the airport and on a direct bus route to the city. (There are campervan rental outlets at the airport.) A Stagecoach day pass is an inexpensive easy way to explore Auckland and can also be used for the ferry to the resort town of Devonport.

The northern part of the North Island has the tranquil **Bay of Islands**, magnificent **Ninety Mile Beach**, and picturesque **Coromandel Peninsula.** About 150 miles south of Auckland are the **Waitomo Caves**, with impressive limestone features and thousands of glowworms, which reflect the underground river. The Glowworm Grotto is best explored by watercraft or (outfitted in wetsuits and cavers' helmets) on inner tubes. The **Te Anau Glowworm Caves** on the South Island are a more accessible alternative to those at Waitomo, which are off the main travel route.

The coastal plateau south of Auckland is the heart of **Maori** culture, the original Polynesian settlers in 800AD. The active volcanic area around **Rotorua**, with boiling mud, hot springs, and steaming terraces of sulphur and silica deposits, is one of the country's most popular attractions. Take in a Maori *hengi* (feast) and concert and the Agrodome **farm show** just outside Rotorua, which was one of the highlights of our trip. (A professional can shear a sheep in one piece in less than two minutes!) **Tongariro National Park** has dramatic mountain/volcanic scenery and good hiking tracks.

The capital city of **Wellington**, often compared to San Francisco, is noted for its harbour, hills, winds, and the **Te Papa Museum**. In 2002 there were no holiday parks close to the downtown area or on a direct bus route, but a campervan could be easily parked in the centrally located parking lot next to the Te Papa (not the main museum parking lot or parkade). An all-day Stagecoach pass in Wellington in 2011 costs $5NZ.

The Wellington-Picton **ferry across Cook Straight**, with Wellington's beautiful harbour, the "near mystical" **Marlborough Sounds**, and possibly schools of dolphin, is one of New Zealand's best travel experiences. A confirmed reservation entitling you to a discount is strongly advised, and an online booking gives further savings. Expect to pay around $350NZ one way for two adults and campervan and expect the three hour trip to be windy and rough.

The South Island

As the larger of the two islands, residents call it "The Mainland". It is also more sparsely populated, somewhat less expensive, and the roads are less busy than on the North Island (another reason to begin your trip in Christchurch). Before or after the ferry, allow time to explore the beautiful beaches and hiking tracks on the northern part of the island. The 51 km **Abel Tasman Coastal Trek**, one of the easiest, can be done in half-day sections. The 71 km **Queen Charlotte Track** out of Picton is also popular. Shuttle services are available.

Kaikoura, on the east coast, with albatross, penguins, whale watching tours, and opportunities to snorkel or swim with dolphins or seals, has been described as one of the world's best eco-tourism destinations. Watch for the **Ohau Point Seal Colony** a few miles north of town (another highlight of our trip). **Hanmer Springs** is known for its thermal pools and spa.

The very English "Garden City" of **Christchurch** has been named by *Travel and Leisure* as #2 of "The Top Ten Cities in the World". We were impressed with its parks, the Avon River, and ambience, but disappointed that the infamous Wizard was not ranting and raving at Cathedral Square as he does frequently on summer afternoons. There are campgrounds on bus routes right in town, Amber Holiday Park personally recommended. The **International Antarctic Center** is located across from the airport. After the 2011 earthquake Christchurch will never be the same.

The southernmost city of **Dunedin** is a student town with Scottish heritage and Baldwin Street, according to *The Guinness Book of Records,* the steepest street in the world. A nearby ecological preserve attracts many visitors, as does the nightly return of the Blue Penguin Colony at **Oamaru.**

Queenstown on Lake Wakatipu has been compared to Banff for its picture-book mountain setting, as well as charges of over-commercialism. With its many extreme sport offerings, it has been called the adrenalin capital of New Zealand. *Lord of the Rings* was filmed in the area.

Queenstown

Mount Cook National Park, with Fox and Franz Josef Glaciers and 12,317 foot Mount Cook, is a favourite destination for climbing and flight-seeing. According to *The Lonely Planet* the 200 kilometre stretch of Route 6 south of Westport on the west coast is rated "one of the top coastal drives in the world". Also, the 145-mile **Tanzalpine Express** from Christchurch to **Greymouth** on the west coast is said to be "one of the great railway trips of the world", but those having traversed the Canadian Rockies by rail will be disappointed.

A cruise on **Milford Sound** is a must, fog and rain adding an ethereal aura to the surrounding mountains but also frequently causing cancellation of flight-seeing over the magnificent west coast. It is recommended visitors take a bus tour from **Te Anau** to avoid driving the narrow Homer Tunnel and challenging mountain roads. The world-famous four-day **Milford Track** must be booked a year in advance and closes in the snowy winter months.

Milford Sound

New Zealand has the mountains and rainforests of British Columbia, verdant pasturelands of Ireland, fjords of Norway, geysers and hot springs of Yellowstone, and beaches of Hawaii. All for the price of one! How can you resist?

VANCOUVER ISLAND—
FOR SCENERY, SAVINGS,
AND POSSIBLE SHOWERS

With the high cost of fuel and out-of-country health insurance, some Canadians opt to spend the winter in the balmiest part of their own country–southern Vancouver Island. To a farmer from Saskatchewan, or even a retired teacher from Chilliwack, the Island winters look pretty good. And with snow-capped mountains, shimmering water, lush rainforests and gorgeous beaches, the setting is –as the B.C. Department of Tourism says—Super, Natural!

Its high temperatures in the 6 degree range, January weather on Vancouver Island can't compare with Palm Springs, Phoenix, Brownsville, Miami, Cabo San Lucas, or Auckland. But there are pansies in January, crocuses in February, green grass all winter, and even a few palm trees here and there. Often there will be showers, but with Gortex you can still enjoy the outdoors. Every few years there's a major snowstorm to add a little excitement and keep the residents of Lotusland from becoming too complacent, but the white stuff doesn't last long.

Why the Island rather than the Lower Mainland around Vancouver? The weather is better–less precipitation, milder temperatures, and more sunlight. (Having wintered in both places I can vouch for it.) Island living is more economical, including park rates, groceries, and usually gas. The lifestyle is more relaxed, with less traffic, pollution, and crime, plus lots of free and easy parking.

On the downside, the ever-increasing **ferry** fares in 2011 are around $50 for a 20' vehicle, plus over $5 per additional foot, and about $14 per person each way, varying with the month and day of the week. Debit cards are not accepted. B.C. seniors sail free Monday through Thursday (but their vehicle doesn't). The Tsawwassen ferry terminal is more accessible traffic-wise for big rigs than the one at Horseshoe Bay.

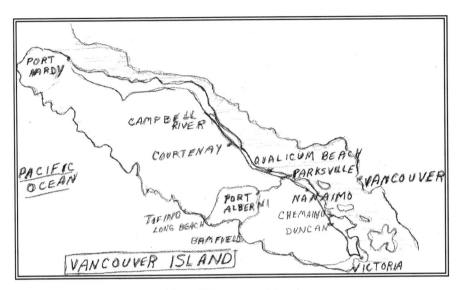

Map of Vancouver Island

The Capital Region

Many snowbirds congregate at Fort Victoria RV Park (off Highway 1 at Exit 8), which has 300 sites and a nearby bus stop to downtown, with the waterfront, Parliament Buildings, Royal British Columbia Museum, and lots of interesting shops, many with British imports and native handicrafts. With its historic buildings, year-round gardens, horse and buggy rides, tea at the Empress Hotel, and bustling harbour, **Victoria** is a delightful city. Beach lovers may prefer to set up base camp at Weir's Beach Resort 15 miles west, still within easy striking distance of the "action".

The Saanich Peninsula's golf courses (between the ferry terminal and the city) are well-used year round, and boating, birding, and cycling are also popular in the area. But the Peninsula's main attraction is the world-famous **Butchart Gardens**, off Exit 18. In addition to side trips by car, a Via Rail dayliner runs between Victoria and Courtney, and ferries depart Victoria for Seattle, Anacortez, and the San Juan Islands in Washington.

The East Central Region

To my mind the best part of Vancouver Island for wintering is the Nanaimo/Parksville area, a central location for all the Island's attractions. It is little more than two hours drive to Victoria to the south, Pacific Rim National Park with magnificent **Long Beach** and its awesome winter storms to the west, the recreation areas of **Strathcona Park** and **Mount Washington** (the only full-service ski resort in North America with an ocean view) to the north, and a sampling of **Gulf Islands** (rated by *Conde Nast Traveler* among the top three non-tropical island destinations in the world) to the east. The nearby towns of **Duncan, Chemainus,** and **Coombs** are renowned respectively for totem poles, murals, and goats on the roof (but not in the winter). The M.V. Frances Barkley cruises out of **Port Alberni**, up and down the picturesque Alberni Inlet to and from Bamfield.

Pacific Rim National Park

In the vicinity are myriad hiking and walking trails and numerous reasonably-priced **golf** courses open fifty-two weeks a year. Check out: Mount Washington if you are a **skier** or a snowboarder (there are 50 runs serviced by eight lifts and 40 km of cross-country trails); Top Bridge Trail if you're a cyclist; Rebecca Spit on Quadra Island if you're a **beachcomber**;   Horne Lakes Provincial Park if you're a **caver** (one of the best sites of its kind in Canada); and the Nanaimo River for bungee-jumping if you are a **thrill-seeker**.

For **nature-lovers** the area abounds with wildlife–notably eagles, herons, deer, and seals. **Birders** will enjoy the nature reserve bordering Surfside RV Resort, plus the stopover of the duck-size Brant geese on their way to Alaska the end of February and the related festivities in March.

Malaspina College in Parksville and Malaspina University of Nanaimo offer Elderhostel, craft, computer, and general interest courses. Both population centers, as well as nearby Qualicum Beach, have bookstores, video outlets, and libraries, plus art galleries, and craft and antique shops. There are seniors' groups, bridge clubs, and branches of the Legion, all of whom probably welcome Winter Islanders. For a cardio workout, there are indoor pools and fitness centers, a variety of community dance groups, and bowling, hockey, and curling leagues.

Nanaimo

In addition to its annual bathtub race (in the summer) and the delectable dessert bars bearing its name, Nanaimo boasts the largest square footage of **shopping** space per capita in North America, as well as an impressive **waterfront**, where cruise ships dock in the summer and walkers do their thing year round.

The city of over 100,000 also has a **casino** and the 800 seat Port **Theater** which presents a full calendar of live entertainment, including various theater and choral groups, a Jazz Fest, the Vancouver Island Symphony Orchestra, the Winnipeg Ballet, and Randy "Elvis" Friske. Nanaimo and Qualicum Beach have local theater groups and Chemainus a dinner theater. Many of Nanaimo's eateries are staffed by students and graduates of Malaspina's culinary arts program. For hockey fans there's the Junior A Nanaimo Clippers.

The award-winning 53 acre Living Forest Oceanside Campground, seven miles south of the city, caters to snowbirds with a cozy "winter lodge" and 50amp and wi-fi sites. Check out their excellent website. To the west of the city is the Resort on the Lake RV Park.

Parksville/Qualicum

Location, location, location. Surfside, Park Sands, and Paradise RV Parks are all located right on beautiful Parksville Bay. Also on the water, nearby Rathtrevor Beach Provincial Park has wonderful forested campsites, difficult to get into in the summer, but available and cheap in the winter.

Parksville and the nearby "Village of Qualicum Beach" (as it likes to be called), offer all the amenities of a small city, but for more extensive shopping and serious medical problems, Nanaimo is only half an hour away. The area has a good selection of **restaurants,** notably Maclure House, Tigh-Na-Mara, Kalvas, China Garden, and Shady Rest.

Qualicum Beach waterfront

Life in the two oceanfront communities (together referred to as Oceanside) is really laid back. The *Police Briefs* section in the local paper typically reports nothing more serious than B and E's where "a box of Cheerios and a yellow flashlight" were stolen (actual quote!).

Campgrounds

There are no 1000-site megaresorts as in the U.S. Sunbelt, but there are lots of trees, grass, mountains, and ocean views. There are fire pits and picnic tables, and TV channels which aren't inundated with U.S. politics. On New Year's Day there are Polar Bear Swims.

You won't have icecream socials, useable outdoor pools, brake seminars with chocolate long johns, or 18-hour line dancing. There won't be on-site facilities for lapidary, silversmith, or ceramics, batting cages, or pickle ball courts. You'll have to leave the park and pay for water aerobics and painting lessons. There'll be no social director to plan your day, but RVers organize their own activities—crafts, games, cards, dances, puzzles, jam sessions, potlucks, etc., in the clubhouse.

Monthly winter rates at Island RV resorts in 2011 range from $450 to $700 (depending mainly on proximity to the water), plus taxes and sometimes electricity. Or you can boondock for $10 a night ($5 for B.C. seniors) for 14 days at Rathtrevor Beach. Just like on the BLM lands down south! Sort of. Just remember when temperatures dip below zero to leave a tap dripping at night to keep waterlines from freezing.

To avoid driving the RV on possible snow-covered mountain roads, consider enjoying Beautiful British Columbia in the summer, putting the rig (and perhaps tow vehicle) in storage, and returning in the fall.

There will be no dust storms, wild fires, tornados, twelve-lane freeways, or toll roads. You'll use more propane up north but save on sunscreen. On outings your doggie can guard the car. You won't have to worry about getting American money or out-of-country insurance. You can bring oranges.

Except for a little rain southern Vancouver Island stacks up well as a snowbird alternative. But beware—a visit to the Island can be risky. It is easy to fall in love with, even in the winter. Few of the Island's residents were born there.

CATCHING THE SPIRIT

As you "catch the spirit" of the RVing lifestyle (to quote author/RVer Peggi McDonald) you will want to learn more about the care and feeding of your rig, new models and accessories, and unvisited parks and destinations. You will be drawn to other RVers and various RV associations and shows.

And once you have experienced semi-tropical winters it is hard to tolerate sub-zero ones. For most, "once a snowbird always a snowbird", for as long as health and money permit, although over the years your snowbirding style will likely change.

(Inter) National RV Organizations

With over a million members, the **Good Sam Club** is the largest organization for RVers. Membership offers 10% camping discounts at over 1700 parks (as listed in the *Trailer Life Directory*), savings on RV parts, accessories, and repairs at many outlets, plus insurance and mail-forwarding options. Good Sam has over 1600 local chapters (including ones in Canada), and hosts frequent "Samborees" (rallies) and "Caraventures" (RV caravan trips).

The **Escapees** (SKP's) group is noted for "members helping members", its mail and telephone forwarding service, and RV retirement park for those who can no long travel but wish to remain in their rigs. It is a close-knit, socially active club, with many sub-chapters ("Birds of a Feather") and rallies. Members, even those meeting for the first time, traditionally greet with a hug. As well as regular "Rainbow Parks" open to the public, the SKP organization has a number of member-owned co-ops with low camping rates, plus reasonably-priced, although seldom available, lots for purchase. The headquarters in Livingston, Texas provides a "home address" for thousands of full-timers in the U.S.–the reason there are so many RV's with Texas license plates.

The **Family Motor Coach Association** offers mail, telephone, and other services and discounts for owners of motorhomes (not trailers or fifth wheels). FMCA membership, shown with a distinctive black decal on the rig, is often included with the purchase of a new coach.

The Ontario-based **Explorer RV Club** offers emergency road service, rallies, safety clinics, and other events; discounts on rental cars, hotels, and campgrounds; and RV, home, auto, and travel insurance. Their bimonthly *RV gazette* magazine can be subscribed to without membership.

The **Canadian Snowbird Association,** although focusing mainly on non-RVing snowbirds in the eastern provinces, is an influential government advocacy group "dedicated to actively defending and improving the rights and privileges of Canadian travelers". It is particularly involved with provincial funding and residency requirements for out-of-country (and out-of–province) health care, policies regarding vacation supplies of prescription drugs, and other transborder issues. It also offers travel (Medipac), medical, home, and auto insurance.

Membership in the above organizations varies from $20 to $90 a year and includes regular magazines.

Rallies, Shows, and Seminars

In your travels you will be exposed to a large variety of **clubs** and interest groups, comprised of residents of certain locales, square dancers, singles, gays, naturists, physically challenged, retired military personnel, owners of RV brands, members of camping membership clubs, and on and on. Often they have catchy monikers such as "BUTTNS"–Bounders United/TTN (Bounder owners who belong to Thousand Trails/NACO), and Indybagos (Winnebago owners from Indiana). Most groups put out a newsletter and hold regular get-togethers.

"**Jamborees**" are large rallies providing opportunities for RVers with similar interests to play and party, as well as attend seminars, exhibits, and entertainment productions. The mother of all RV jamborees is **The Rally,** put on annually in the early summer by the parent company of the major suppliers of RV goods and services, including Camping World, Good Sam, and Coast to Coast. In 2011 the event costs $149 to $369 per unit for three days and expects about 5000 rigs, quite an increase from the first documented RV rally of 20 Tin Can Tourists (so-called because they ate out of tin-cans), who met at DeSoto Campground near Orlando in 1919.

The Canadian Snowbird Association presents annual winter "**CSA Extravaganzas**" in Lakeland, Florida; South Padre Island, Texas; Mesa, Arizona; and Indio, California. Admission is free.

Large cities have regular RV **trade shows,** mainly for dealers to present new models and to sell off old ones, but also including seminars and booths promoting products, clubs, and destinations. The Vancouver area offers three such shows, including one in September catering to snowbirds.

The **RV Owners Lifestyle Seminar** is held annually over three days at the end of June at Okanagan University College in Kelowna (250 762-5445). The popular **Life on Wheels** conferences, presented for many years at college campuses around the U.S., were discontinued with the passing of its founder Gaylord Maxwell in 2008.

Keep current on shows, seminars, and rallies, as well as trends in RVing by reading the various trade publications. Western Canada's *RV Times* also provides an extensive list of coming events in B.C., Alberta, and Washington, as well as classified ads and letters, a wide variety of articles, and a vicarious friendship with editor Sheila Tourand. The *Times* is published bimonthly and available in most western Canada RV outlets and all Kal-Tire locations, Overwaitea and Save-On Food stores in British Columbia and Alberta; plus Lordco, Thrifty Foods, visitor centers, many campgrounds, and numerous other outlets in B.C.; as well as several locations in the Yukon. For free! (Or by subscription.) It is required reading for RVers in Western Canada.

Home is Where You Park It

Many RV snowbirds are happiest on the open road, exploring new territory, visiting a grand array of resorts, and making friends out of strangers they meet en route. After much soul-searching, increasing numbers are deciding to cut ties with their old life in the city and take on a new one where the world is their back yard. In the United

States an estimated two to three million have decided to sell or rent their homes and, armed with maps and multiple campground memberships, become full-time RVers. In Canada too, although more restricted, "full-timing" is gaining in popularity.

The major hurdle for Canadian wannabe full-timers is the half-time residency requirement to maintain our valuable **provincial health care** coverage. (For information on individual provincial requirements check out the Canadian Snowbird Association website at snowbirds.org.) Residency is not met by touring around the province-of-choice for the six months you are not down south.

Canadian fulltimers/lifestyle consultants Peggi and John McDonald write:

> *We RVers may put our head down wherever we choose but we must be a legal resident of a province to reap benefits such as medical coverage–we need official addresses/residences that we call home. In provinces such as British Columbia, RVers residing long-term in a campground can use that address as their official residence–this can be a lot you purchased or one you lease. In other provinces an official residence must become your home base–this can be a house that you own, an apartment or a room at the house of a son or daughter or relative. A mailbox or a campground address is not sufficient. Be advised that officials at the border are asking more questions these days; however, they mainly want to be reassured that you have a reason to return home... Although you should never lie, you should never volunteer the fact that you are full-timing.*

Many B.C. full-timers own **RV lots** at Holiday Park in Kelowna, SunKatcher RV park near Keremeos, Tapadera Estates near Chilliwack, Caravans West on Shuswap Lake, and Surfside RV in Parksville–good places to hang out from mid-April to mid-October.

Canadian full-timers often stay down south the maximum six months. Out-of country **health insurance** is expensive, but you must not leave home without it. (See chapter on *Taking Care of Business*.)

Insurance for full-timers' RV contents, ordinarily covered on a home policy, is offered through the Explorer RV and Good Sam Clubs, as well as the Aviva Insurance Company.

If you are out of Canada more than an average of four months a year, you are required to fill out an **IRS form** proving a closer connection to Canada. The official number of days is more than 182 in three years, based on the formula—each day in the present year counts as a full day, in the previous year a day counts as 1/3 of a day, and two years back a day counts as 1/6 of a day. For more information on the subject, check out the snowbirds.org website or get Publication 519, a U.S. Tax Guide for Aliens.

Full-timers can use a **mail-forwarding** system, such as that offered by Canada Post, the UPS Store, FedEx Office, or Good Sam, but some RV parks do not accept mail. The alternative is General Delivery, where you arrange for forwarding when you know you will be in one spot for awhile. Most long-term RVers now correspond by e-mail and cellphone, and use automatic withdrawals, telephone banking, or the Internet to pay bills.

Be prepared for major **downsizing** and emotional upheaval if you choose to become a full-timer. It will be difficult deciding what to sell or give away, what to put in storage, and what to take with you. Decisions will vary according to whether you plan to sell or rent out your house, and for how long you plan to be happy wanderers. Full-timers often purchase a larger rig.

Non-RVers do not understand the appeal of the nomadic lifestyle. Your friends and relatives will think you have gone out of your mind if you trade your 2000 square foot home for a 240 square foot cubicle on wheels. During our two years as full-timers in our brand new 35' Bounder, we were considered "homeless" by family members. Your children and parents will not like you to "disappear" for long periods. On the plus side, offspring of fulltime RVers do not move back home.

We met a number of Canadian full-timers—all delighted with their new life. One couple spends summers on the B.C. coastal waters in their Bayliner and winters in the Sunbelt in their 36' Alpenlite fifth wheel, using their daughter's address as a home base. Another summers on their lot at SunCatcher in Keremeos. A third has a condo in Lethbridge, although is seldom there.

Don't jump into it. Discuss the pros and cons, especially with those who have taken the big step. Try it out for a few months. But if you love RVing and traveling and don't require large living quarters (keeping in mind that metal shrinks when wet), then why not? The real world will still be there when you decide to return.

When Getting There is no Longer Half the Fun

In the beginning it is fun to explore the various Sunbelt attractions and to check out the different state parks, private resorts, and public camping areas. The time may come, however, when you find a park where you like to return each year–where the ambience, the people, and the amenities are just right.

But getting there can be stressful. Driving a fifty-foot, multi-ton load, especially down long mountain grades, in poor visibility, on slick pavement, or battling Santa Ana winds, doesn't get easier with age. And watching the meter as you fuel up is not good for your blood pressure. For those who have come to dislike the long drive to their winter playground there are several options.

Professional drivers advertise in RV publications, and for easterners, the Amtrak AutoTrain will transport your RV from Lorton, Virginia to Standford, Florida. A more common choice is to store the RV at the favourite snowbird park for the summer months and travel to and from in the easy-to-drive car or truck. You will save big-time on fuel, although there will be motel and restaurant bills, plus storage fees. Or you can fly to your stored RV and rent a gadabout vehicle. In the latter case research airfares and rental rates thoroughly, as prices vary greatly.

The main disadvantage of southern storage is, of course, that you cannot use the RV during the rest of the year. Sunbelt storage lots have mainly trailers and fifth-wheels, whose owners often have a second inexpensive RV up north. If you leave a Canadian-purchased recreation vehicle in the U.S. for more than a year you are required to fill out documents for importation.

The most popular choice for northerners turned off the long haul and fuel costs, is to buy or rent a **park model** or trailer at that special Sunbelt park, or buy offsite and set up at the chosen park. The average cost of a new 400 square foot park model is about $30,000, although resales in snowbird hotspots are plentiful and a used 20' trailer can often be purchased for under $5000. You will get the best deal on a purchase at the end of snowbird season. It will then cost about $1500 to $3000 a year to lease a site, plus there are insurance and taxes. Friends paid around $3500 annually a few years back to keep their park model in a resort near Casa Grande, Arizona.

Be sure you are thoroughly familiar with park regulations and income tax implications before you make such a commitment. Also, consider that in Florida because of high humidity there are mould and mildew problems with homes locked up for the summer, plus the threat of hurricanes, and the Phoenix area has termites. Florida also has high non-resident property taxes.

In 2011 there are some really good real estate offerings in the United States. Some RV snowbirds may consider switching to a condo in their favourite Sunbelt location, but most prefer to remain in the RV community.

Whatever their lifestyle choices, snowbirds recognize that the grass is usually greener on the northern side of the fence, but in winter the sun is warmer on the southern side. The game plan is to enjoy both worlds to the max.

RV TALK

AARP - American Association of Retired Persons

AC - air conditioning

AC Current - alternating current (from shore power or a generator)

Affinity Group - former parent company of Good Sam, Coast to Coast, Camp Club USA, Camping World, *Trailer Life*, *Woodalls*, The Rally, and other RV-related ventures

AOR - Adventure Outdoor Resorts

Back-up Camera - (rear view camera) transfers an image of the area behind the motorhome to a monitor on the dashboard

Black Water - toilet sewage

BLM Lands - public land operated by the U.S. Bureau of Land Management

Boondocking - camping with no hookups (dry camping)

California Duster - a feather duster specially treated to remove desert sand from a vehicle

Camping World - a retail outlet for RV supplies

Caravan - a group of RV's traveling together

CARP - Canadian Association of Retired Persons

Casitas – small houses

Catalytic Heater - uses propane rather than electricity

CCC - Coast to Coast CampResorts

ccc - cargo carrying capacity

Chassis - driver controls—including transmission, driveline, engine, brakes, steering, suspension, electrical accessories

Converter - changes alternating current from the landline or generator to direct current

CRA - Colorado River Adventures

CSA - Canadian Snowbird Association

CTC - Coast to Coast

Dinghy - a vehicle towed by a motorhome

DC Power - direct current power (from the battery)

Dry Camping - camping with no hookups (boondocking)

Dry Weight - weight without passengers, fuel, cargo, and accessories

Dump Station - a drive-up location where waste water tanks can be emptied

ELS - Equity LifeStyles—an investment/realty company with numerous resort retirement parks mainly in the Sunbelt, owner of Thousand Trails

Escapees - SKP's (acronym for support, knowledge, parking), a large RV club

Fan-Tastic Fan/Vent - a ceiling fan which can be operated from the coach battery and shuts off at a pre-selected temperature (Magic Fan)

Fifth Wheel - a type of trailer with a raised front which hangs over and attaches onto a truck box

Fiver - a fifth wheel

FMCA - Family Motor Coach Association

Full Hookups - water, power, and sewer

Full-timer - person who lives in an RV year-round

GAWR - (gross axle weight rating), the carrying capacity of each axle

GCWR - (gross combined weight rating), maximum weight of the towing vehicle and towed vehicle, plus the load of each

Generator - an engine which provides backup power

Genset - a generator

Grey Water - water from sinks, bathtubs, and showers

GVWR - (gross vehicle weight rating), the maximum allowable weight of a loaded motor home or trailer (with passengers, fuel, cargo, and accessories)

Honey Wagon - a truck which serves as a mobile dump station

Hook Up - attach to a power and water source and sewer outlet

House Battery - provides 12 volt electricity to the RV

Inverter - changes direct current from batteries to alternating current to power appliances when there is no shore power

Kelley Blue Book - an automotive vehicle evaluation manual

LP, LPG - liquefied petroleum gas (propane)

LTVA - Long Term Visitor Area

Medium Duty Truck - an outsized heavy duty truck used for towing large fifth wheels

Mobile Home - a modular home set-up permanently in a park

NADA - National Automobile Dealers' Association

Net Weight - weight of an empty vehicle

ORA - Outdoor Resorts of America

Park Model - a small mobile home

Pocketmail - a mini-computer used with a telephone to access and send e-mail, once popular with Rvers, is no longer in service

Pusher - having the engine in the rear

Rally - a gathering of RVers with similar interests

Rear View Camera/Monitor - a backup camera/monitor

Rig - recreational vehicle (RV)

RPI - Resort Parks International

Shore Power - electricity from an external source

Slideout, Slider - an extension of the living area which slides out from the original body of an RV

SKP's - Escapees

Skype - a software application which allows users to make voice calls over the Internet and also video conferencing

Solar Panels - roof attachments which use sun to help keep house batteries charged

Sunbelt USA - RV membership Club associated with WHR

TA - Travel Centers of America (travel plaza)

Tailgunner - the last RVer in a caravan

Tote-Along Tank - portable plastic tank with 5 to 32 gallon capacity used for storing and transporting waste water

Toad - a towed vehicle

TTN - Thousand Trails/NACO

Umbilical Cords - power cord and hoses used in hooking up

Wagonmaster - the leader in a caravan

Walmart SuperCenter - has a complete grocery department, often open 24/7

WHR - Western Horizon Resorts

Wi-Fi - wireless fidelity, not requiring a phone line to connect to the Internet

CHECK IT OUT—BOOKS AND WEBSITES

BOOKS

Abraham, Marilyn J., First We Quit Our Jobs, 1997.

Baker, Kim and Sunny, The RVers Bible, 1997.

Barre, Harold, Managing 12 Volts, 2002.

Bourie, S.; Burton, B.; Curtis, A; Dancer, B.; American Casino Guide, 2007.

Cadieux, Charles L., Great RV Trips, 1998.

Church, Mike and Terri, Traveler's Guide to Mexican Camping, 2005.

Church, Mike and Terri, Traveler's Guide To Mexico's Baja, 2006.

Counts, David and Dorothy, Over the Next Hill, 2001.

Cumming, Andrew, Florida Bound; The Essential Guide for Canadian Snowbirds, 1999.

Davin, D.J., RV Camping in State Parks, 2007.

De Maris, Russ, RV Boondocking Basics, 2004.

De Vos, Robert and Brice, Tracie, RVers Friend (overnight parking and dump stations, America's truck and travel plazas), 2007.

Edwards, Marianne, The Frugal Shunpiker's Guides to Boondocking.

Estes, Bill, RV Handbook: the Essential How-to Guide for the RV Owner, 2000.

Farlow, Bill, several titles.

Gallant, J.D., How to Select, Inspect, and Buy an RV, 2000.

Gelbert, Doug, The Canine Hiker's Bible, 2004.

Gray, Douglas, The Canadian Snowbird Guide, 2007.

Groene, Janet and Gordon, <u>Living Aboard Your RV</u>, 2001.

Henkle, S.L., <u>Camping With the Corps of Engineers</u>, 2005.

Hossack, Joei Carlton, several titles.

Hunter, Dave, <u>Along Florida's Expressways</u>, 2008.

Hunter, Dave, <u>Along Interstate 75</u>, 2006.

Kenny, Jane, <u>Casino Camping</u>, 2004.

Johnson, Carlean, <u>6 Ingredients or Less</u> (3 titles), 1989, 2002, 2004.

Livingston, Bob, <u>Trailer Life's RV Repair and Maintenance Manual</u>, 2008.

Mackintosh, Graham, <u>Into a Desert Place: a 3000 Mile Walk Around the Coast of Baja California</u>, 1995.

Maxwell, Gaylord, <u>Fulltiming: an Introduction to Full-Time RVing</u>, 1998.

McDonald, Peggi, <u>RVing in the 21st Century</u>, 2004.

Miller, Richard, <u>Mountain Directory</u> (East and West Editions), 2006.

Moore, M.; Dubocq, T; Denien, S.; and MacLure, R.; <u>Foghorn Outdoors Florida Camping</u>, 2000.

Obivos, Kathy, <u>Mexico by RV</u>, 2002.

Peterson, Walt and Michael, <u>Exploring Baja by RV</u>, 1996.

Posner, Stan and Phillips Posner, Sandra, <u>Drive I-95</u>, 2007.

Stienstra, Tim, <u>Foghorn Outdoors California Camping</u>, 2003.

Wallis, Michael, <u>The Mother Road</u>, 2001.

Warren, Scott S., <u>100 Hikes in Arizona</u>, 2007.

Watson, Mark, <u>The Next Exit</u>, 2011.

Williams, Jack and Patty, <u>Fielding's Baja California</u>, 1997.

Wright, Don, Guide to Free Campgrounds, 2007.

Wright, Don, How to Buy an RV and Save Thousands, 2004.

Zikman, S.; Hall, J.; and Zyetz, A., RV Traveling Tales: Women's Journeys on the Open Road, 2003.

*   *   *

Trailer Life Directory

Trailer Life Directory RV Road Atlas

Woodall's Campground Guide

Exit Now Interstate Exit Directory

All are available on Amazon.com.

WEBSITES

amazon.com (for books)

aorcamping.com

arizonaguide.com

blm.gov/az (Arizona BLM)

busnuts.com (camperized buses)

ca.blm.gov (California BLM)

campclubusa.com

camphalfprice.com (Happy Campers RV Club)

cbp.gov (U.S. Customs)

coastresorts.com (Coast to Coast)

coloradoriveradventures.com

explorer-rvclub.com

freetrip.com

geocaching.com

holidaytrailsresorts.com

kiwistyletravel.com (New Zealand RV rentals)

kmresorts.com

mexico.com

nadaguides.com

newzealand.com/travel

passportamerica.com

remcotowing.com

resortparks.com (RPI)

resortsofdistinction.com

rv.net

rv.org (RV Consumers' Group)

rvadvice.com

rvbookstore.com

rversonline.org

rvliving.net

rvparkreviews.com

rvparkstore.com

rvschool.com (driving)

rvtimes.com

sanidumps.com

snowbirds.org (CSA)

thousandtrails.com

vancouverisland.com

visitcalifornia.com

visitflorida.com

visittex.com

weather.com

westernhorizonresorts.com

wififreespot.com

INDEX